Steck Vaughn

Maps Globes Graphs

Teacher's Edition

Level B

Contents

Meet your state standards with free blackline masters and links to other materials at
www.HarcourtAchieve.com/AchievementZone.
Click Steck-Vaughn Standards.

ISBN 0-7398-9108-1

© 2004 Harcourt Achieve Inc.

Rigby • Steck-Vaughn

www.HarcourtAchieve.com
1.800.531.5015

About the Program

Steck-Vaughn *Maps•Globes•Graphs* has been developed to teach important geography and social studies skills in a six-level program. Up-to-date, in-depth information in a self-contained format makes this series an ideal supplement to basal texts or an excellent independent social studies skills course. Clear, concise maps present new concepts in a straightforward manner without overwhelming students with too much information. As students develop practical skills, such as map interpretation, they also develop the confidence to use these skills. The features incorporated into the *Maps•Globes•Graphs* program were developed to achieve these goals.

Maps•Globes•Graphs consists of six student books with accompanying annotated Teacher's Editions. The series is organized as follows:

Book	Level
Level A	Grade 1
Level B	Grade 2
Level C	Grade 3
Level D	Grade 4
Level E	Grade 5
Level F	Grade 6

STUDENT EDITION FEATURES

◆ **Consistent formats** for each chapter include two teaching pages that introduce the skill, two practice pages, one mixed practice page, and *Skill Check*, a review page.

◆ **Geography Themes Up Close** introduces the five themes of geography—location, place, human/environment interaction, movement, and regions—in the beginning of the book. These themes are reinforced in five two-page special features that emphasize the concepts and relevance of the themes.

◆ *Map Attack!* and *Graph Attack!* features (in the three upper-grade books) build general understanding of interpreting map and graph information in a step-by-step format.

◆ **Vocabulary** words highlighted in bold type emphasize in-context definitions and increase understanding of the terms critical to studies in geography.

◆ **Glossaries** in each student book serve as both an index and a resource for definitions of key terms.

◆ **Atlas maps** in each book are a valuable reference tool for instruction and study.

TEACHER EDITION FEATURES

◆ **Annotated** Teacher's Editions facilitate effective instruction with minimal preparation.

◆ **Scope and Sequence** reflects key concepts of basal instruction for each grade level.

◆ **Teaching strategies** identify key objectives and vocabulary for each chapter and provide suggestions for introducing skills, teaching specific lesson pages and concepts, following up lessons with extension activities, and enhancing concept mastery with activities to complete at home.

◆ **Extension activities** involve both cooperative learning and critical thinking, and reinforce the concepts and skills taught in the program.

♦ **Geography themes teaching strategies** reinforce geography skills and vocabulary through lesson introductions, teaching notes, and extension activities.

♦ **Blackline Masters** further supplement the activities available for use:

Map Attack! may be used with maps in a basal text or in reference materials.

Outline maps appropriate to each grade level may be used for skills practice in map labeling and place recognition.

Activities and *games* reinforce concepts.

Standardized tests in each level allow students to check their learning, as well as practice test-taking skills.

Steck-Vaughn Company grants you permission to duplicate enough copies of these blacklines to distribute to your students. You can also use these blacklines to make overhead transparencies.

♦ **Transparencies** provide full-color instructional aids. These transparencies may be used to introduce lessons, to reinforce key map and globe skills, or to review chapter concepts. These transparencies are perforated in the back of the teacher's editions for easy removal.

♦ **Letters to Families,** in English and in Spanish, are provided in each book. The letters invite families to participate in their child's study of the book and provide suggestions for some specific activities that can extend the concepts presented in the program.

SUGGESTIONS FOR PROGRAM USE

Maps•Globes•Graphs is easy to implement in any classroom. The following suggestions offer ways to adapt the program to particular classroom and student needs.

♦ Alternate the *Maps•Globes•Graphs* chapters with chapters in the social studies program. After presenting your first social studies chapter, present the first chapter of *Maps•Globes•Graphs*. When you return to the regular social studies program, apply any map skills learned to maps that appear in the curriculum. In this way, students reinforce their new skills in a variety of contexts.

♦ Set aside a specific time each week for map study. For example, spend half an hour every Friday on map study. Do as much in the *Maps•Globes•Graphs* Worktext® as time permits. Related activities, such as map show and tell, could be included in the map study time.

♦ Focus on a complete chapter of map study and cover the entire program at the beginning of the year, at the end of the year, or whenever best fits your class schedule.

The map and globe chapters in *Maps•Globes•Graphs* progress developmentally. For this reason they should be taught in the order they are presented in the Worktext®. However, the last chapter in each book presents several types of graphs, so this chapter could be interspersed with map chapters. In Levels D, E, and F, the graph topics reflect subjects covered by the maps and the basal programs. The graphs also can be used in conjunction with the graph presentation in mathematics studies.

Meet your state standards with free blackline masters and links to other materials at **www.HarcourtAchieve.com/AchievementZone**. Click **Steck-Vaughn Standards**.

Scope and Sequence

Numbers refer to the chapters where each skill is first taught. These skills are reviewed and reinforced throughout the book and the series, as well as in the "Geography Themes Up Close" special features.

		LEVEL A	LEVEL B	LEVEL C	LEVEL D	LEVEL E	LEVEL F
Map Recognition	Photo/Picture Distinction	1, 2					
	Photo/Map Distinction	3	2		1		
	Map defined	3	2	1	1		2
Map Key/Legend	Pictorial symbols/Symbol defined	6	2	1	1	2	
	Labels	7	7	1	1	2	2
	Legend defined and related to map	6	2	1	1	2	2
	Abstract symbols		2, 3, 6	1, 3	1	2	2
	Political boundaries		6	1	1	2	2
Direction	Top, Bottom, Left, Right	4					
	North, South, East, West	5	3	1	1	1	1
	Relative location	4–7	3–6	1–6	1–8	1–5, 7, 8, 11	2–5, 10
	Compass rose		3	1	1	1	2
	Cardinal directions (term)				1	1	2
	Intermediate directions			1	2	1	2
Scale and Distance	Miles/Kilometers/Map Scale/Distance			2	4	3	3
	Mileage markers				5	4	4
Latitude and Longitude	Equator		4	7	7	8	1, 6
	Latitude			7	7	8	6
	Degrees			7, 8	7	8	6
	Longitude/Prime Meridian			8	8	9	6
	Estimating Degrees				7	8, 9	6
	Parallel					8	6
	Meridian					9	6
	Latitude and Longitude					9	6
The Globe	Globe	7	4	7, 8	7, 8	1	1
	North Pole/South Pole		4	8	7, 8	1, 8–10	1
	Continents/Oceans		4, 5	7, 8	7, 8	8, 9	1
	Northern/Southern Hemispheres			7	7	8	1
	Eastern/Western Hemispheres			8	8	9	1
	Tropics of Capricorn/Cancer					8	7
	Arctic/Antarctic Circles					8	7

		LEVEL A	LEVEL B	LEVEL C	LEVEL D	LEVEL E	LEVEL F
Grids	Grid Coordinates/Map index			6	3	7	4
Graphs	Pictograph			9			
Graphs	Bar Graph			9	9	12	12
Graphs	Line Graph			9	9	12	12
Graphs	Circle Graph			9	9	12	12
Graphs	Time Line			9	9		
Graphs	Flow Chart			9	9		
Graphs	Tables					12	12
Landforms	Types of Landforms		1	4	6	5	5
Landforms	Landform Maps			4			
Landforms	Relief Maps				6	5	5
Landforms	Physical Maps/Elevation					5	5
Types of Maps	Route Maps			5	5	4	4
Types of Maps	Resource Maps			3	1		9
Types of Maps	Special Purpose Maps				1	6	8, 9
Types of Maps	Combining Maps/Comparing Maps						8, 9
Types of Maps	Historical Maps					6	
Types of Maps	Climate Maps						7, 8
Types of Maps	Land Use Maps						9
Types of Maps	Inset Maps		7			3	3
Time Zones	Time zones defined					11	10
Time Zones	International Date Line						10
Temperature Zones	Low latitudes					10	7
Temperature Zones	Middle latitudes					10	7
Temperature Zones	High latitudes					10	7
Temperature Zones	Sun/Earth relationship					10	7
Projections	Projections defined						11
Projections	Mercator						11
Projections	Robinson						11
Projections	Polar						1, 11

OBJECTIVES

Students will
◆ identify the five geographic themes: location, place, human/environment interaction, movement, and regions
◆ describe locations using relative terms
◆ describe the features of places that make them different from other places
◆ give examples of how people interact with the environment
◆ identify movement of people, goods, and ideas
◆ recognize the characteristics of regions

VOCABULARY

location	human/environment
place	interaction
movement	regions

INTRODUCING THE FIVE THEMES OF GEOGRAPHY

◆ In 1984 a joint committee of the National Council for Geographic Education and the Association of American Geographers published the *Guidelines for Geographic Education: Elementary and Secondary Schools*. This publication outlined the five fundamental themes in geography—location, place, human/environment interaction, movement, and regions. These themes help geographers and geography students organize the information they gather as they study Earth and its people.

◆ **Location** is the position of people and places on Earth. There are two ways to describe location—absolute location and relative location. Absolute location is described using a specific address based on a grid system. Latitude and longitude is the absolute location of a place based on the intersection of lines of latitude and lines of longitude. Relative location describes a location in relation to what it is near or what is around it. One example of using relative location is by giving directions. How would you tell a friend to get to your house from the local library? The special feature about location is on pages 42 and 43.

◆ **Place** tells what the location is like based on two kinds of features—physical features and human features. Physical features are part of the natural environment, such as soil, landforms, climate, and plant and animal life. Human features include those created or developed by people, such as roads, buildings, governments, religion, playgrounds, schools, and other elements of culture. The special feature on place is on pages 50 and 51.

◆ **Human/Environment Interaction** describes relationships within places. It describes the interaction of people and their environment—how people adapt to and/or change their environment. For example, people in areas with frequent hurricanes might use special building materials to withstand the effects of hurricanes. People cut down trees and clear the land to farm. The special feature about human/environment interaction is on pages 14 and 15.

◆ **Movement** describes the way people, goods, information, and ideas move from one part of Earth to another through transportation and communication. Movement is the study of the interdependence of people, the linkages between places. The special feature on movement is on pages 28 and 29.

◆ **Regions** are the basic units of geographic study. Regions are a way to organize information about areas with common features. Geographers use physical and human features as criteria to draw regional boundaries. Some physical features include climate, landforms, bodies of water, and animal life. Some human features include land use, language, political units, and population. Regions can be as small as a classroom or as large as a continent. The special feature on regions is on pages 58 and 59.

TEACHING NOTES

Pages 4–7   Read and discuss the activities with students. Point out to students that they will learn more about the five ways to study geography in special features called "Geography Themes Up Close" throughout *Maps•Globes•Graphs*.

EXTENSION ACTIVITY

◆ Divide the class into five groups—one group for each of the five themes. Ask students to use newspapers and magazines to find examples in pictures, advertisements, and stories that relate to their theme. Students can assemble their findings in a chart, concept map, or poster.

1 Land and Water

OBJECTIVES

Students will
◆ identify common land and water features

MATERIALS NEEDED

travel brochures, magazines
Transparencies 1, 2
index cards
maps of your state, butcher paper
flour, salt, cream of tartar

VOCABULARY

island	mountain
lake	plain
river	ocean
valley	landform
hill	

INTRODUCING THE SKILL

◆ Tell students Earth is made up of land and water. Explain that they will be learning about some of the land and water forms on Earth. Ask students to think of how land and water forms are used by people. Possible answers: mountains for skiing; valleys and plains for farming; lakes and rivers for drinking water, recreation, etc. Make a chart to show students' ideas.

◆ Have students name the land and water forms found near their school.

◆ Go to a travel agency to get old brochures or collect magazines with pictures of various land and water forms. Have students work with a partner to cut out pictures and make one collage of landforms and another of water forms.

TEACHING NOTES

Pages 8 and 9 Use Transparencies 1 and 2 as you work with students to introduce the concepts on these pages. Discuss the various land and water forms in the photos on pages 8 and 9. Have students compare the land and water forms by asking how a mountain is different from a hill or how a lake is different from a river or an ocean. Next, ask students to circle the photo of the place they would most like to visit.

Page 10 Before students color the land and water forms, help them identify these places. Direct students to circle an island, make a fence around part of the plain, mark an **X** in the lake, draw a line under the label for the valley, circle the labels for mountains, draw a triangle next to the label for hills, and draw an arrow from the river label into the ocean.

Page 11 Have students use the glossary on pages 63 and 64 and write each word from the word list on page 11 on a separate index card or small sheet of paper. Help students put the cards or sheets in order according to the alphabetical order of the words. Then have students look up the words in the glossary and write a definition for each. Students may enjoy drawing pictures of the land and water forms under the definition, or they can cut out the drawings from the glossary (with the exception of the ocean) and paste them under their definition.

Page 12 Have students draw a red line down the trail to show the route they will take from the mountains to the beach.

Page 13 If students need extra practice, have them identify various land and water forms in pictures from magazines, geography books, or picture books.

EXTENSION ACTIVITIES

◆ Divide the class into cooperative learning groups. Provide each group with a large sheet of white butcher paper and a map of your state. First, have students use a black marker to darken the outline of the state on the map. Next, have students attach the butcher paper on top of the map and trace the outline of the state. Help them identify any major land and water forms in the state. Then have them draw and label land and water forms on their butcher-paper map. Make sure students consider the following land and water forms: mountains, hills, plains, valleys, lakes, rivers, islands, and oceans. Display the finished maps on the wall.

◆ Take a field trip to a nearby land or water form. After returning to the classroom, have students illustrate what they saw and write one or two sentences describing the trip.

◆ Divide the class into groups. Have students mix together 2 cups flour, $1/2$ cup salt, 2 tsp. cream of tartar, and 1 cup water. Ask them to knead the mixture and place it on a board, then shape it into plains, hills, mountains, valleys, rivers, lakes, oceans, and islands. Allow several days for the salt maps to dry, then have students paint the land and water forms with tempera paints.

AT HOME ACTIVITY

◆ Make a list of the eight land and water forms studied in this unit. Have students take the list home and invite a family member to help them draw pictures to illustrate four of the land or water forms on the list. Ask students to label their land or water forms, and ask them to share their drawings with the class.

OBJECTIVES

Students will
◆ identify ways people adapt to their environment
◆ identify ways people change the land

MATERIALS NEEDED

pictures or photographs of various environments on Earth

VOCABULARY

human/environment interaction

INTRODUCING THE SKILL

◆ Discuss with students the definition of the word *environment.* (*Everything around us—the land, water, air, plant life, and animal life.*) Call on students to describe the environment of their neighborhood. Ask students to describe other environments, like the mountains, an island, an arctic environment, and so on. Explain to the class that in this feature they will learn how people live in their particular environment.

TEACHING NOTES

Page 14   Read and discuss with students the introductory paragraph on page 14. Ask students what they do differently during each season of the year or in different weather. Do they wear different clothes? Do they play different sports? Do they eat different foods or prepare them differently, such as grilling them outdoors? Lead students to realize that when they make these changes they are *adapting* to, or learning to live in, their environment. Then, expand the discussion. Show students pictures of different environments, such as the Arizona desert, the arctic, a tropical island, and so on. Ask students how people adapt in these environments. For example, depending on where people live, what kinds of homes do they build? How do they get from place to place?
◆ Have students work the exercise on page 14. Discuss their answers. Ask students for other examples of how people make changes in dress and recreation from season to season.
Page 15   Explain to students that although people change to live in their environment—like wearing warmer, heavier clothing in winter—people also

make changes to the environment. Read the introductory paragraph with students. Then have students complete the activity on the page. Ask volunteers to share their drawings. Discuss the drawings in number 8. Use this as a springboard for discussing how the environment of their neighborhood affects how they live.

EXTENSION ACTIVITIES

◆ Have students look at the map on page 56. Point out to students that the land and water forms of a place affect people. Ask: How do the Rocky Mountains and the Appalachian Mountains affect the lives of the people who live there? How do they affect people in the following ways: making a living, having fun, getting around, the number of people who live there? (*It is difficult to farm in mountain areas. There are trees for lumber, paper, etc. in the mountains, so people could make a living in the lumber business. People can ski in mountain areas. Mountains make transportation difficult because it is hard to build roads and railroads. Few people live in mountain areas because it is hard to make a living and get around there.*) Next, ask: How do rivers affect the lives of people who live near them? How do they affect people in the following ways: making a living, having fun, getting around, the number of people who live there? (*People can use rivers to fish. They can use rivers to water farm crops. People can use rivers for boating, fishing, and swimming. People can use rivers to get from place to place. Rivers, however, may make it difficult to get around because you cannot cross them except where there are bridges. Many people tend to live near rivers because they are helpful for farming, having fun, and transportation.*)
◆ Have students draw pictures of how the seasons in their environment shape the way they live. For example, they might draw a picture of children swimming at a neighborhood pool in summer. Display the drawings on a bulletin board entitled: "Seasons Change the Way We Live."

AT HOME ACTIVITY

◆ Have students work with family members to observe and describe ways the school neighborhood might be changed to improve its appearance or make it safer. Have students share their descriptions with the class.

OBJECTIVES

Students will
* compare an aerial photograph with a map
* use a map key to read symbols on a map
* determine relative location

MATERIALS NEEDED

Transparency 3
aerial-view photos or drawings
Blackline Master T21
newspaper weather maps
map of your state, construction paper

VOCABULARY

photo   symbols
map   map key

INTRODUCING THE SKILL

* Show students aerial-view photos or drawings, and discuss the difference between ground-level and aerial points of view. Have students identify objects in the aerial views.
* Take students on a field trip to a high point in the community, such as a scenic overlook, mountain or hill, top of a building, elevated walkway, etc. Have students record their observations, noting what they saw from the high point and what they saw at a lower level. Discuss how an overhead view compares with a ground view. Discuss reasons for not showing everything on a map.
* Have students identify symbols they use at school (+, −, =, $, and 0 for add, subtract, equals, dollars, and cents). List familiar symbols such as color on traffic lights, various road signs, and holiday symbols like pumpkins, turkeys, and hearts. Then have students make up symbols for common items.
* Have students practice identifying symbols on map keys using maps found in the classroom, the library, or in basal textbooks. Ask them to find matching symbols on the maps.

TEACHING NOTES

Page 16 Use Transparency 3 as you introduce the concepts on this page.

Pages 16 and 17 Have students compare the photo of the town on page 16 with the map on page 17. Discuss how they are different. Examples: the photo shows each building as a different color, cars on the streets, and cars in parking areas. Ask students why the map would not show all of these details. (Accept any reasonable answers.) Direct students to look at each symbol, read its label from the map key on page 17, and locate each symbol on the map. Then have them use the photo on page 16 to locate the real objects represented by symbols.

Pages 18 and 19 Divide the class into cooperative learning groups. Take students on a walk through the school neighborhood. Direct students to find at least three things that they could represent with a symbol. In the classroom, have students draw, color, and cut out their symbols. Then provide each group with a large sheet of construction paper. In the center of the paper, have students draw a symbol for the school. Ask them to create a map of the neighborhood by pasting their symbols around the school.

Page 20 Tell students that they will draw a map of the school playground. First, take students to visit the playground. Then have them brainstorm a list of all the objects found on the playground. Write the list on the chalkboard for students to refer to for correct spelling. Ask students to draw a map with symbols to show the location of objects on the playground. Tell them to include a map key with a symbol and a label for each object.

EXTENSION ACTIVITIES

* Give students copies of the symbols blackline on page T21. Have students draw maps of their neighborhood with a map key. Students may draw their own symbols or use the ones from the symbols blackline on page T21.
* Bring several weather maps from different newspapers to class for students to examine. Discuss the various symbols on the map keys and compare the different symbols used on the maps for the same weather conditions. Have students make a variety of weather symbols. Place a large map of your state or the United States on a bulletin board. Have students start each school day by taking turns being weather forecasters and pinning the appropriate symbols on the map.
* Have students work in small groups to create treasure maps with a map key. Direct them to make symbols for places that would be passed on the way to the treasure, such as a lake, mountain, cave, or forest. Students should include an **X** in the key and on the map to show where the treasure is hidden. Give each group a large sheet of construction paper to draw their map using the symbols and adding directions to find the treasure. Have the groups exchange maps and directions and then solve each other's treasure maps.

AT HOME ACTIVITY

* Have students work with a family member to create a map of a room in their home. Tell them to be sure to include a map key that shows symbols for the items found in that room, such as a sofa, chair, lamp, TV, etc.

OBJECTIVES

Students will
◆ locate cardinal directions on a compass rose and on a map
◆ recognize abbreviations (N, S, E, W) for north, south, east, and west
◆ determine relative location

MATERIALS NEEDED

compass
Blackline Masters T21, T22-T23, T24, T27
Transparency 4
aerial-view photos or drawings
newspaper weather maps
map of your state, construction paper

VOCABULARY

north   west
south   directions
east   compass rose

INTRODUCING THE SKILL

◆ Show students a compass, and explain how it is used. Let students discover that the compass will always point to the north. Have students use the compass to find and label the cardinal directions in the classroom. Have students brainstorm a list of things found in each cardinal direction.

◆ Have copies of the scarecrow blackline on page T21 ready for students to color, cut out, and paste down in the center of a large sheet of construction paper. Direct students to label the cardinal directions and draw pictures of things found in each direction in the classroom or outside.

◆ Provide students with copies of the compass rose blackline on page T24. Have students follow the directions to make the game spinner. Divide the class into pairs of students. Ask students to take turns spinning the direction arrow. Have them identify the direction and then name something in the classroom or in the school that is found in that direction.

◆ Provide students with the blackline map of the United States on page T27. Have students label and color two or three states in each of the cardinal directions. Students may wish to refer to the atlas map of the United States on page 60.

TEACHING NOTES

Page 22   Take students outside to a sidewalk or paved area on the playground. Using a compass and several different colors of chalk, draw the outline for three or four compass roses similar to the one in the picture on page 22. Divide the class into three or

four groups. Have students color each compass rose with the chalk and label the four cardinal directions with N, S, E, and W. Have them take turns standing in the center of their compass rose while you call out a direction. Have the student in each compass rose name an object in that direction. Continue playing until every student has had a turn.

Page 23   Use Transparency 4 with students as you work through the exercises on this page.

Page 24   If students have difficulty with cardinal directions, you may wish to give them additional practice before progressing to page 25, which introduces relative location.

Page 25   Help students to locate Main Street on the map. Ask them which symbols are to the east of Main Street. Then ask which are to the west. Repeat with First Avenue and Second Avenue by asking students to identify symbols that are north and south of each avenue.

Page 26   Have students create a symbol for a lake and then draw that symbol west of the river. You may wish to have students create other symbols and add them to the map in places that you specify.

Page 27   Discuss with students other symbols that could be placed on the map. Make a list on the chalkboard with a simple symbol next to each suggestion. Have students choose one of the symbols, add the symbol and its label to the map key, and then draw the symbol south of the post office on the map.

EXTENSION ACTIVITIES

◆ Play the game "I Spy" for things in the classroom, using cardinal directions in your clues. For example, the clue might be, "I spy something that is blue and west of the bulletin board."

◆ Divide the class into small groups. Have students work together to make a compass. Have them rub a tapestry or embroidery needle several times with a magnet. Be sure they rub in only one direction. Have them place the needle on a piece of cork or sponge 1 inch square and $1/4$-inch thick. Then have them place the cork or sponge in a bowl of water. The needle will point to the north.

◆ Give students copies of the blackline campsite map on page T22 and the corresponding symbols and directions on page T23. You can use this activity as a review of chapter skills.

AT HOME ACTIVITY

◆ Direct students to ask a family member to help them draw a map of their street, home, or a room in their home with the four cardinal directions labeled on the map.

Geography Themes Up Close

OBJECTIVES

Students will
- identify symbols on maps for roads, highways, airports, and other transportation routes
- explain how people, goods, information, and ideas get from place to place in neighborhoods and in a country

MATERIALS NEEDED

road atlas

VOCABULARY

movement

INTRODUCING THE SKILL

- Ask students to fold a piece of paper in half. On one half of the paper have them list all the ways they traveled in the past week. On the other half of the paper, have them list all the ways they learned new information and ideas. Give them the following example to help them think of ideas: "You learned new information and ideas when you read this book. You learned new information and ideas when you talked to your friend on the telephone." Call on volunteers to read their lists. Start with the "transportation" lists. Continue calling on volunteers until there are no new answers. Do the same with the "communication" lists. Tell students that in this feature they will learn more about the movement of people, goods, information, and ideas.

TEACHING NOTES

Page 28 Have students read the introductory paragraph. Then have them complete questions 1–3. Discuss the answers with students. Emphasize that the map shows only some of the highways in some parts of the United States. Point out that the map does not include the states of Hawaii and Alaska. Use a road atlas to show students the highways in Alaska and Hawaii. Ask questions similar to those on page 28 about the highways in these two states.
- Ask students to name routes or ways other than highways that people and goods can use to move throughout the United States. (*Airports, railways, waterways, canals, pipelines*)

Page 29 Have students describe how the map on this page is different from the map on page 28. (*The map on this page shows a neighborhood. The map on page 28 shows part of the United States.*)

- Have students complete questions 4 and 5. Discuss the answers with students. Ask students: How do you get to school? How do your parents get to work? How does your family get to the supermarket and other stores? How do you and your family get to places to have fun?
- Read the paragraph on ideas on page 29 with students and have them complete question 6. Have them discuss their answers. Point out that any answer involving communication is correct.

EXTENSION ACTIVITIES

- Have students draw pictures of several kinds of vehicles that could be used to travel from one point to another in the neighborhood.
- Have students evaluate the best means of transportation to move the following goods or people from place to place: books from home to the library; groceries from the store to home; oil from oil wells to a gas station; a person from California to Idaho; coal from mines to factories, timber from forests to sawmills; mail from one state to another state.
- Have students brainstorm several ways available in their community to send a message to another person in the community, to someone in a different community in their state, to someone in another state, and to someone in another country.
- Have students compare and contrast the kinds of vehicles used to move people and goods today and long ago (100 years ago). Have students share their findings. They might organize their findings in a time line.
- Have students identify classmates who have moved to their school from other places. Have them locate those places on a local map, a map of the state, a map of the United States, or a world map, whichever is appropriate.
- Have students draw a map of their neighborhood (including the location of their home) and surrounding community. The map should have major roads and highways and places that provide important goods and services.

AT HOME ACTIVITY

- Have students work with family members to make a list of places they travel to in one week. Have them keep track of the means of transportation they use to get to all these places. Then have students share their lists with the class.

OBJECTIVES

Students will
◆ recognize and locate the continents and oceans
◆ identify the Equator, North Pole, and South Pole

MATERIALS NEEDED

globes
Blackline Masters T21, T25
Transparency 5

VOCABULARY

globe	Antarctica
ocean	Pacific Ocean
continent	Atlantic Ocean
North America	Indian Ocean
South America	Arctic Ocean
Australia	Equator
Africa	North Pole
Europe	South Pole
Asia	

INTRODUCING THE SKILL

◆ Divide the class into small groups. Have students use a globe to locate the four oceans and seven continents.
◆ To give students an easy way to visualize their location on Earth, draw a small person on heavy paper with tabs below the feet. Cut the person out and fold one tab forward and one tab back so that your person can stand up. Tape the person above your location on the globe.
◆ Divide the class into cooperative learning groups. Provide groups with copies of the symbols blackline on page T21 and a globe. Have students use the cut-out car, boat, and plane from page T21 to take imaginary trips between places on the globe. Ask them to name the direction of travel.
◆ Use copies of the globe blackline on page T25. First, make one as a model. Then have each student color and cut out a globe. Help students glue their globe together at the North Pole and South Pole. Have them tape tab A to side B to form a sphere. Help them add tape at the poles to make their globe sturdy. Ask students to find the continents, oceans, and their own location on their globe.

TEACHING NOTES

Page 30   Show students a globe with labels for the continents, oceans, countries, etc. Have them compare and contrast the globe with the inset photo of Earth on page 30. First, ask how they are the same. (*They both show that Earth is round and made up of water and land.*) Then ask how they are

different. (*The globe uses labels and is shown in different colors than the real Earth. In addition, clouds appear on the photo but not on the globe.*)
Page 31   Use Transparency 5 with students to introduce the concepts on this page.
Page 32   Show students the Equator on a globe and on the illustration of the globe on this page. Have them circle the label in red. Explain that the Equator is an imaginary circle that divides Earth in half. Next, point out the North Pole and the South Pole on the globe. Explain that the poles are the very top and bottom places on Earth. To demonstrate these concepts, use an orange or grapefruit. Show students the stem and tell them this represents the North Pole. Turn the fruit over and show them the bottom, which represents the South Pole. Now take a knife and cut the fruit in half between the top and the bottom to show the Equator.
Page 34   To give students additional practice with finding directions on a globe, ask them which ocean is east of Asia (*Pacific Ocean*), which continent is north of Africa (*Europe*), and which ocean is north of North America (*Arctic Ocean*).

EXTENSION ACTIVITIES

◆ Divide the class into two teams to play "Spin the Globe." Have students take turns gently spinning the globe and then placing a finger on the globe to stop it. Students must name the ocean or continent beneath their finger to score a point for their team. Then ask students directional questions, such as "Which ocean is east of your finger?" or "Which continent is south of your finger?"
◆ Have students blow up large balloons and cover them with papier mâché. After the papier mâché has dried, have students paint and label the oceans and continents to make a globe. Ask them to mark and label the Equator and the poles.
◆ Have students make a globe for an imaginary planet, using clay, a Styrofoam ball, or papier mâché. Ask students to add places with name labels on their globe. Then have students write a story about their planet.

AT HOME ACTIVITY

◆ Direct students to ask a family member to help them find a newspaper or magazine article about a country, continent, or ocean. Encourage students to have the family member read and explain the article to them so that they can report on it to the class. Have students hang their article on a bulletin board entitled, "Current Global Events." Invite students to bring additional articles to class that they can report on and add to the bulletin board.

OBJECTIVES

Students will
◆ compare a globe with a flat map
◆ identify continents and oceans on a world map

MATERIALS NEEDED

globe	butcher paper
world map	heavy paper
Blackline Master T29	large envelope
Transparency 6	

VOCABULARY

globe	Antarctica
continent	Pacific Ocean
ocean	Atlantic Ocean
North America	Indian Ocean
South America	Arctic Ocean
Europe	North Pole
Africa	South Pole
Asia	Equator
Australia	

INTRODUCING THE SKILL

◆ Have students locate the North and South poles on a globe or world map. Explain that there is land at the South Pole. Ask what continent is found at the South Pole (*Antarctica*). Explain that there is not any land at the North Pole, but freezing temperatures keep the water frozen as ice, forming a polar ice cap.

◆ Provide students with copies of the blackline map of the world on page T29. Have students label the continents and the oceans.

◆ Use the blackline map of the world on page T29 to play a game of "I Spy," with the oceans and continents. Examples: "I spy with my little eye a continent north of Africa," or "I spy with my little eye an ocean west of Europe."

TEACHING NOTES

Page 36 Use Transparency 6 to introduce the concepts on this page. Have students compare a globe and a flat world map. If possible, have globes and flat world maps available for students to examine. Lead students to conclude that the map and globe are similar because they both show land and water on Earth. Be sure students note the following differences: a globe is round and a map is flat; only half of Earth can be seen at a time when looking at a globe, but the entire Earth can be seen when looking at a flat world map.

Page 37 Help students draw and label the Equator and the North and South poles on the map on page 37. Student may wish to use the map at the bottom of page 36 as a reference.

Page 38 Ask students to name the two continents that are completely north of the Equator (*North America, Europe*). Then ask what ocean is east of Africa (*Indian Ocean*). Have students circle the pole that is located on a continent (*South Pole*). Have students make an **X** on the pole that is located on frozen ice without any land (*North Pole*).

Page 40 Write *sphere* on the chalkboard. Explain that Earth is a sphere, or shaped like a ball. Next, write *hemisphere* on the chalkboard. Circle *sphere* and review its meaning, Tell students that *hemi* means *"half"* and that each half of Earth is called a *hemisphere*. Direct students to look at the map on page 40. Explain that the half of Earth between the Equator and the North Pole is called the Northern Hemisphere, and the half of Earth between the Equator and the South Pole is called the Southern Hemisphere. Next, direct students' attention to the dotted line on the map on this page. Explain that if an imaginary line is drawn from the North Pole to the South Pole, two other hemispheres are created. The half of Earth to the east of the line is the Eastern Hemisphere, and the half of Earth to the west of the line is the Western Hemisphere. Help students to identify various continents and oceans in each of the four hemispheres.

EXTENSION ACTIVITIES

◆ Select stories from different countries to read orally to the class. Have students look at a world map to determine in which continent the countries are located.

◆ Ask your librarian to select age-appropriate materials about the continents of the world. Divide the class into seven groups. Assign one continent to each group. Ask each group to give an oral presentation about their continent. Students may wish to illustrate what their continent looks like, trace a simple map, or discuss what kind of wildlife lives on their continent.

◆ Make an overhead transparency of the blackline map of the world on page T29. Project the transparency onto butcher paper. Have students help you trace, color, and label the continents and oceans. Laminate or paste the map on another sheet of heavy paper to make it sturdy. Cut the map into pieces to make a puzzle. Challenge students to put the puzzle of the world together. Store the puzzle in a large envelope for students to use as an independent activity.

AT HOME ACTIVITY

◆ Give students a copy of the blackline map of the world on page T29 to take home. Have students ask a family member to help them locate and label the name of the countries from which their ancestors came.

Geography Themes Up Close

OBJECTIVES

Students will
◆ locate places relative to other places on a world map
◆ use grids to identify the exact locations of places

MATERIALS NEEDED

Blackline Master T27
maps with grids (optional)

VOCABULARY

location
grid

INTRODUCING THE SKILL

◆ Ask students to describe where they are sitting in the classroom. Discuss with students the kinds of words used to describe where they are sitting. Write the descriptive words and phrases on the chalkboard. Some of the descriptive words and phrases students may use include *near, by, next to, across from, in front of, in back of.* Explain to students that in this feature they will learn more about how to describe the locations of places.

TEACHING NOTES

Page 42 Have students read the introductory paragraph on this page. Then have them complete questions 1–3. Next, call on students to read their answers to the questions on this page. Have students describe the locations of Montreal, Temuco, Santos, and Salto. You might also ask: What cities are south of the Equator? (*Santos, Temuco, Salto*) What city in South America is west of Salto? (*Temuco*) What city is closest to the North Pole? (*Fairbanks*)
◆ Give students copies of the blackline map of the United States on page T27. Give them additional skill practice by having them locate and label the state capitals starred on the map. Have them refer to the atlas map on page 60. For example, you might say: Label the capital of Pennsylvania, which is directly north of our nation's capital (*Harrisburg*).
Page 43 Read the information in the first paragraph on this page with students. This may be their first introduction to grid systems. Help students understand grid systems. Make a copy of a grid, like the one on this page, on the chalkboard. (Do not include the map.) Using the grid on the chalkboard, show students that the

squares going across the grid form rows labeled A, B, C, and D. Tell students: Put your finger on Letter A. Move your finger across the row to the other Letter A. All these squares are in Row A. Next, show students that the squares going down the grid form columns labeled 1, 2, 3, 4, 5, 6, and 7. Tell students: Put your finger on Number 1. Move your finger down the column to the other 1. All these squares are in Column 1. Next, show how each square is in a row and a column. Then draw a triangle in square D-4. Explain to students, as you demonstrate, that the triangle is in row D and in column 4. Tell students that the location of the triangle is square D-4. Draw a star in another square and call on a volunteer to explain to the class the location of the star. Continue with this activity until you are fairly certain that students grasp the concept of a grid system.
◆ Have students complete questions 4–7. Check their answers. Then ask students to find the locations of the other continents and oceans. (*Europe A-4; Asia B-6; South America C-2; Africa C-4; Antarctica D-4; Pacific Ocean C-1 or B-7; Indian Ocean C-5 or C-6.*) You might do this activity with the class or with small groups of students who have not yet understood the grid system.

EXTENSION ACTIVITIES

◆ Give students extra practice with finding the location of places on maps with grids. Have students look at the map on page 23. Point out that the streets form a grid on the map. Then have students label the rows A, B, and C (on both sides of the grid). Next, have them label the columns 1, 2, and 3 (on both the top and the bottom of the grid.) Then have them tell the location of the following: tree (*B-1*); park (*B-2*); library (*C-2*); apartment building (*B-3*). You might also have students draw a tree in squares A-1 and C-3 and a house in square A-3.
◆ Read students a story that talks about locations, such as *Jack and the Beanstalk.* After reading the story to students, have them draw a map that shows how Jack got to the castle.

AT HOME ACTIVITY

◆ Have students work with family members to find the location of their home on a local map. Students might find local maps on the Internet, in the library, or in local phone books. Ask students to tell what their home is near or what is around it. Ask them to write down their home address.

OBJECTIVES

Students will
♦ identify and locate capital cities, state boundaries, and national boundaries on a map
♦ use symbols for boundaries and capitals

MATERIALS NEEDED

globe
world map
Blackline Masters T24, T27, T28
tape or glue
blue yarn
wood or heavy cardboard
color-headed straight pins or push pins
Transparency 7
butcher paper
map of the United States with major rivers

VOCABULARY

boundary	national capital
state boundary	North America
capital city	United States (U.S.)
national boundary	Mexico

INTRODUCING THE SKILL

♦ Provide students with copies of the blackline map of the United States on page T27. Have students locate their state, trace their state boundary, color the state and list all states that form the boundary line with their state.
♦ Provide students with copies of the compass rose game spinner blackline on page T24 and the blackline map of the United States on page T27. Have students make the spinner and use the map to play the "See the U.S.A." game with a partner.

TEACHING NOTES

Page 44 Ask volunteers to locate their home state, the three major countries in North America, the Atlantic Ocean, and Pacific Ocean.

Page 45 Use Transparency 7 to introduce the concepts on this page. Make sure students understand that although Alaska and Hawaii are separated from the other forty-eight states, they are still part of the United States. Have students find Alaska and Hawaii on the map on this page. Explain that Hawaii is part of the United States, but not part of North America. Then, have students work together in groups to practice finding national boundaries, state boundaries, and national capitals on a globe or world map. Place a world map on a bulletin board. Have volunteers locate a state boundary, national boundary, or national capital and mark it with a color-headed straight pin or push pin. Ask students to identify the states or

nations that the boundary separates or the name of the national capital.

Pages 46 and 47 Give students copies of the blackline map of North America on page T28. Call students' attention to the atlas map of North America on page 61 to use as a reference. Direct students to add labels for the countries, national capitals, and oceans to the map. Then have students add a key to the map that matches the key on page 46. Have them color the map to match the key.

Page 48 Have students circle their own state on the map on page 48. Direct them to write an *N* to the north of their state, write an *S* to the south, write an *E* to the east, write a *W* to the west.

Page 49 Make a transparency of the blackline map of North America on page T28. Project the map on a large piece of white butcher paper. Then, ask for volunteers to mark and label the three major countries, national boundaries, and national capitals on the butcher paper.

EXTENSION ACTIVITIES

♦ Find a large map of the United States that shows major rivers. Demonstrate to students that rivers sometimes form state or national boundaries. Tape or glue pieces of blue yarn along the Mississippi, Ohio, Rio Grande, Columbia, and Colorado rivers. Ask students to name states with boundaries formed by these rivers. Ask them if these boundary lines are usually straight or curved (*curved*). Ask which river forms part of a national boundary (*Rio Grande*). Then ask what other water forms create boundaries for states or countries (*Atlantic Ocean, Pacific Ocean, Great Lakes*).
♦ Divide the class into cooperative learning groups. On a large piece of wood or heavy cardboard, have students draw an outline of their state. Discuss important landforms and help students mark them on the board. Have students mix together 2 cups flour, $\frac{1}{2}$ cup salt, 2 tsp. cream of tartar, and 1 cup water. Ask them to knead the mixture and fill in the outline of their state. After the map is dry, have students mark where their community is located. Have them paint the boundary lines and the rest of the map. Also direct students to label neighboring states and other important features.

AT HOME ACTIVITY

♦ Give students copies of the blackline map of the United States on page T27. Have them ask a family member for help identifying and labeling on the map the states they have visited. Have them color those states and then circle one state they would like to visit again. Encourage volunteers to tell why they would like to visit the state they circled.

Geography Themes Up Close

OBJECTIVES

Students will
- identify and describe the features of places using maps
- identify physical and human features on a map
- recognize why places are different from one another

MATERIALS NEEDED

pictures or photos of neighborhoods
a sand table, modeling clay, or drawing paper and
  crayons

VOCABULARY

place

INTRODUCING THE SKILL

◆ Give students five minutes in which to draw the block where their school is located. Students should indicate things such as the school building, playground, houses, and other things on the block. When time is up, call on students to share their drawings. Then ask how this block is different from the block on which they live. Explain that in this feature, they will learn more about what makes each place special and different from any other place.

TEACHING NOTES

Page 50 Read and discuss with students the introductory paragraph on this page. Then have students complete questions 1–3. Call on volunteers to share their answers to question 3. Then ask students how Kenji's neighborhood is like their neighborhood. Next, create a Venn diagram on the chalkboard to compare and contrast students' neighborhoods with Kenji's neighborhood, using students' answers to question 3 and to the question you asked. This activity will help students visualize the concept of place.

◆ Have students look at the map of Green Hills Playground, on page 20. Ask: How is this playground different from a playground that you visit? (*Answers will vary, but should contrast features shown on the map with features of the playgrounds that students visit.*)

Page 51 Read and discuss with students the paragraph at the top of the page. Make sure students understand the difference between "things from nature" (physical features) and "things that people build" (human features). Ask students to name examples of each. Have students study the map and answer the questions on this page. Then discuss their answers. Point out that

Tami's neighborhood has features that make it unique from any other place.

◆ Give students additional practice reviewing the concepts of physical and human features. Ask students to identify natural features in their neighborhoods. Ask them to identify features in their neighborhoods that were made by people.

◆ Have students identify unique places in or near their neighborhoods, such as factories, colleges, amusement parks, business centers, and so forth. Ask: What makes each of these places different from any other place?

EXTENSION ACTIVITIES

◆ Provide students with pictures of neighborhoods. Ask students to identify the physical features and human features in each picture of a neighborhood. Ask students to share their findings with the class.

◆ Have students make a model of an imaginary neighborhood using a sand table, modeling clay, or drawing paper and crayons. Ask students to explain the features of their neighborhood. Display the models in the classroom.

◆ Ask students to draw pictures of the weather in their community during different seasons. Tell them that the kind of weather a place has is a natural feature of the place and that weather helps tell about the place.

◆ Have students create a television advertisement about their neighborhood. The advertisement should tell people why their neighborhood is a good place to live. Have students present their advertisements to the class.

◆ Have students list and compare classmates' feelings about places people have built in their neighborhood or community. For example, they may list and compare their feelings about new streets, buildings, shopping centers, schools, or parks.

AT HOME ACTIVITY

◆ Tell students that the people who live and work in a place make the place special. Have students work with family members to interview several people who live or work in the neighborhood or community to find out about them. Have students write three questions to ask people in their interviews. Then have students, accompanied by a family member or other adult, arrange to interview the selected people. Ask students to tape record or video record their interviews. Then have them share their interviews with the rest of the class.

Map Labels

OBJECTIVES

Students will
◆ use labels to identify states, countries, oceans, and continents on a map
◆ recognize inset maps

MATERIALS NEEDED

map of your state
construction paper: purple, orange, yellow, and green
Blackline Masters T26, T28
Transparency 8

VOCABULARY

title   inset maps

INTRODUCING THE SKILL

◆ Divide the class into small groups. Provide each group with a copy of your state map. Then explain to students that the size of a label on a map or globe generally correlates to the size of the place. The larger the place, the larger the label identifying that place will be. Direct students to locate their community on their group's map. Ask students to compare the size of this label to other labels on the map. Then ask them to find and name the largest label on the map.
◆ Have purple, orange, yellow, and green construction paper available for students to use. Direct students to choose their favorite state from the atlas map of the United States on page 60. Have students design a special label for the state they choose, using construction paper that matches its color on the map. Have students present their labels to the class and tell why they chose that state. Discuss why map labels are important.
◆ Provide students with copies of the blackline map of North America on page T28. Have them label and color the main bodies of water and the three main countries. If students have difficulty with this activity, direct them to use the atlas map of North America on page 61 as a reference.

TEACHING NOTES

Page 52   Direct students' attention to the state labels shown on the globe pictured on page 52. Explain that some states are labeled with an abbreviation instead of a full name.
Page 53   Use Transparency 8 with students as you work through the exercise on this page. After students have drawn a box around their state label according to the directions, challenge them to find their state and circle it in red on the globe on page 52.
Page 54   Call students' attention to the Great Lakes. Ask them to name the eight states with a boundary formed by one of the Great Lakes (*New York, Pennsylvania, Ohio, Indiana, Illinois, Michigan, Wisconsin, and Minnesota*).
Page 55   Ask students why they think the labels for Canada and Mexico are larger than the state labels. (*Canada and Mexico are countries.*) Ask if their title for this map should be larger or smaller than the labels for Canada and Mexico.
Page 56   Divide the class into cooperative learning groups. Provide each group with a map of your state. Have students find labels identifying rivers, lakes, and mountains on the map. Have them make a list of these land and water forms.
◆ For additional practice, give students copies of the blackline landform map and cut–and–paste picture labels on page T26. You may want to have students refer to the atlas map of the United States on page 60. Help students cut out the labels. Then, use directions to have students paste the labels or write a label on various items on the map. For example, say: "Find the label on the map for the Rocky Mountains in the western part of the country. Paste a mountain range picture label there." Repeat this process for the Appalachian Mountains and the Great Salt Lake. Then tell students where there are forests and have them paste the forest picture label in the correct locations. Then say: "Find the river that forms the border between Mexico and Texas. Write the label Rio Grande on this river."

EXTENSION ACTIVITIES

◆ Have students work with a partner to draw a map of their school. Ask them to use labels of different sizes to identify the places on their map.
◆ Divide the class into small groups. Provide a map of your state to each group. Have students study the state map and list any towns or cities that are also the names of people. Challenge students to see if they can find a name matching someone in the classroom, such as Sharon or Allen, or a town name that includes someone's last name, such as Smithville. Have students brainstorm a list of famous cities from around the world, such as Paris and London. Make a list of these cities on the chalkboard. Direct students to see if they can find the names of these cities in their state.

AT HOME ACTIVITY

◆ Encourage students to ask a family member to help them make a simple map of their home or a room in their home. Explain that they should label each room if they draw the entire house, or they should label different items if they draw their room. Have students create an appropriate title for their map. Invite volunteers to share their maps.

Geography Themes Up Close

OBJECTIVES

Students will
◆ define regions as parts of Earth that are alike
◆ identify the features used to name regions
◆ draw inferences from charts about regions
◆ recognize that neighborhoods can be regions

VOCABULARY

regions
chart

INTRODUCING THE SKILL

◆ Have students look at the pictures on pages 8 and 9 in *Maps•Globes•Graphs*. Point out to students that these pictures show different kinds of land surfaces on Earth. These land surfaces are also called landforms. Ask students to use the pictures on pages 8 and 9 to help them brainstorm ways in which the following landforms are different from one another: an island is different from a lake; a valley is different from a river; a mountain is different from a hill; a mountain is different from a plain; an ocean is different from a river. Then point out to students that geographers use landforms as a way of dividing Earth into parts. Explain that in this feature they will learn about some other ways Earth is divided into parts or *regions*.

TEACHING NOTES

Page 58   Read and discuss with students the introductory paragraphs on page 58. Discuss with students what makes mountains, plains, and oceans different from one another. If necessary, refer students back to the definitions of these words on page 9. Emphasize that the shape of the land is one way a region is alike. Another way is the kinds of plants and the kinds of animals that live there.
◆ Help students read the chart. 1) Have students point to the word *Regions* on the chart. Ask them to slide their finger down this column and find the pictures of mountains, plains, and oceans. Point out that this column shows what regions are used in the chart. Continue this same procedure with the column of plants and the column of animals. 2) Again have students find the picture of mountains in the chart. This time, have students slide their finger across the row. Call on students to tell what plants and animals are in mountain regions. Continue this same procedure with the rows that have pictures of plains and the ocean.

◆ Next, have students answer the questions on page 58. Discuss their answers. You may want to point out to students that birds live in all three regions but the types of birds in each region vary. Also point out that some animals that live in mountains can live in plains but not in oceans.
Page 59   Ask students to explain what makes up a neighborhood. Ask students to describe their neighborhood. What kind of buildings do they find there besides houses? Where do people work in the neighborhood? Where do they play? Have students read the introductory paragraph. Point out to students that their neighborhood is a region. Explain that all neighborhoods share certain features. Have students compare their neighborhoods. How are places in a neighborhood alike? How are all neighborhoods alike?
◆ Have students complete the questions on page 59. Call on volunteers to share their responses.

EXTENSION ACTIVITIES

◆ Discuss with students the kinds of regions you might find in a community, such as shopping areas, business districts, park or playground areas, and so on. Discuss ways the places in each of the regions are alike. For example, point out that in a business area, most of the places are providing goods or services. In a playground area, there are places to play or equipment to play on.
◆ Have students work in small groups to make a list of ways their neighborhood is different from a business area in the community.
◆ Have students draw or collect pictures from magazines that represent all the different kinds of workers in their neighborhood. They could do the same for places people play in the neighborhood. Then assemble the pictures on a bulletin board or a collage entitled, "People Work and Play in Neighborhoods."

AT HOME ACTIVITY

◆ Have students work with family members to draw a picture of their neighborhood. Ask them to write a sentence that tells how their neighborhood is a place to live, work, and play. You might suggest to students that they include all the different kinds of workers in their neighborhood in their picture.

Date _____

Dear Family:

Throughout the school year, your child will be learning and practicing geography skills by using *Maps•Globes•Graphs, Level B*. In the seven chapters, your child will work with maps and learn to read symbols, labels, and directions, to identify boundaries, and to locate places like our state. Your child will also learn basic landforms such as mountains, hills, valleys, plains, rivers, lakes, and oceans. In addition, your child will learn to identify the continents.

You can help your child reinforce what we study by asking him or her to talk to you about what we are doing. You might ask your child to explain to you some of the pictures and maps in the book.

You can also help your child by engaging in the following activity at home to support and reinforce our study of these skills.

• Find maps in newspapers or magazines and discuss them with your child. Discuss any symbols on the map. Help your child identify and understand what is shown on the map. Additionally, work with your child to make simple maps of your neighborhood, the area around your school, place of work, place of worship, or shopping area. Be sure to indicate directions and include symbols for items you show on your maps.

Thank you for your interest and support.

Sincerely,

_____

Carta a las Familias

Fecha _____

Querida familia:

A lo largo de este año escolar, su hijo o hija aprenderá y practicará destrezas de geografía usando *Maps•Globes•Graphs, Level B*. En los siete capítulos, su hijo o hija trabajará con mapas y aprenderá a leer símbolos, rótulos y direcciones para identificar límites y para localizar lugares en su estado. Su hijo o hija también aprenderá relieves básicos como montañas, colinas, valles, llanuras, ríos, lagos y océanos. Además él o ella aprenderá a identificar los continentes.

Usted puede ayudar a reforzar lo estudiado pidiendo a su hijo o hija que la cuente lo que hacemos en la escuela y que le explique algunos de los dibujos y mapas en el libro.

Usted puede ayudar a su hijo o hija en casa con la siguiente actividad.

• Encuentre mapas en periódicos o revistas y discútalos con su hijo o hija. Hablen sobre los símbolos que ven en los mapas. Ayude a su hijo o hija a identificar y entender lo que se muestra en el mapa. También trabaje con su hijo o hija para hacer mapas simples de su barrio, la zona alrededor de la escuela, su lugar de trabajo, su lugar de oración o la zona comercial. Asegúrense de indicar direcciones e incluir símbolos para cada detalle mostrado en sus mapas.

Gracias por su interés y apoyo.

Sinceramente,

_____

Name _____

SCARECROW AND SYMBOLS

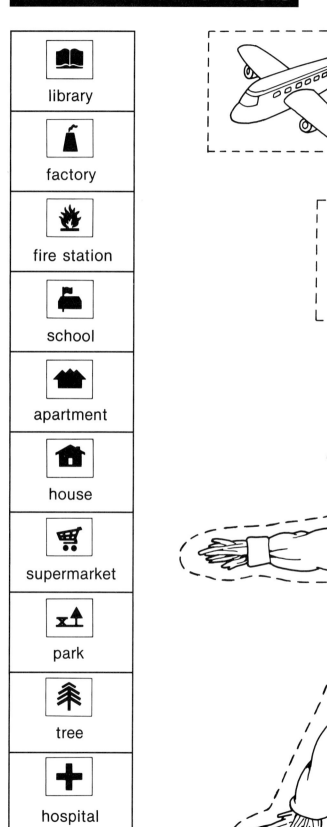

library

factory

fire station

school

apartment

house

supermarket

park

tree

hospital

Name

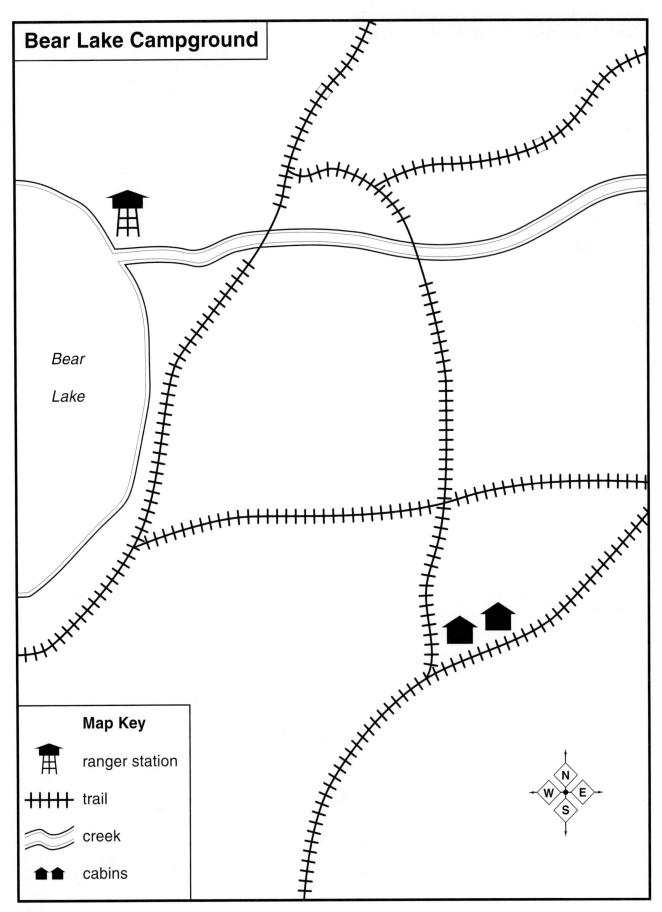

Bear Lake Campground

Bear

Lake

Map Key

ranger station

trail

creek

cabins

N
W · E
S

Maps•Globes•Graphs   Level B

Name _____

Bear Lake Campground

Directions

1. Cut out the symbols for Bear Lake Campground.

2. Paste trees south of the lake.

3. There is one ranger station near the lake. Paste another ranger station on the campground near the three trails and two cabins.

4. Paste the food hall and the first aid station west of the cabins.

5. Paste the picnic area south of the creek and east of the marked trail.

6. Paste the boathouse south of the creek on the east edge of the lake.

7. Paste all other symbols where you think they go on the map.

trees	cabins	bridge	first-aid station	canoe
trees	cabins	bridge	boat house	picnic area
trees	play area	ranger station	food hall	campfire

Name _____

COMPASS ROSE GAME SPINNER

| 1 | 2 | 3 | 4 |
| red | green | blue | orange |

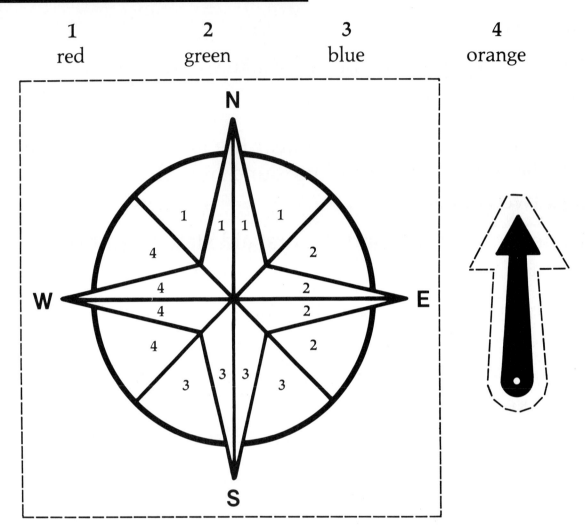

Directions for Making Game Spinner

Color compass rose by number. Cut out and mount on a piece of cardboard. Cut out and mount the black spinner arrow on a piece of heavy paper. Attach the arrow to the compass rose with a brass fastener.

Play "See the U.S.A." Game

Number of Players: 2 to 4

Materials: the compass rose game spinner
a map of the United States (page T27)
a different color crayon for each player

Directions: Start in Kansas.
Spin the compass rose needle.
Move one state in the direction on the spinner.
Color the state with your crayon.
Look at the map on page 60 and name the state.
The next player takes a turn.

The player who has colored the most states is the winner.

  Maps•Globes•Graphs   Level B   © Harcourt Achieve Inc. All rights reserved.

Name _____

GLOBE

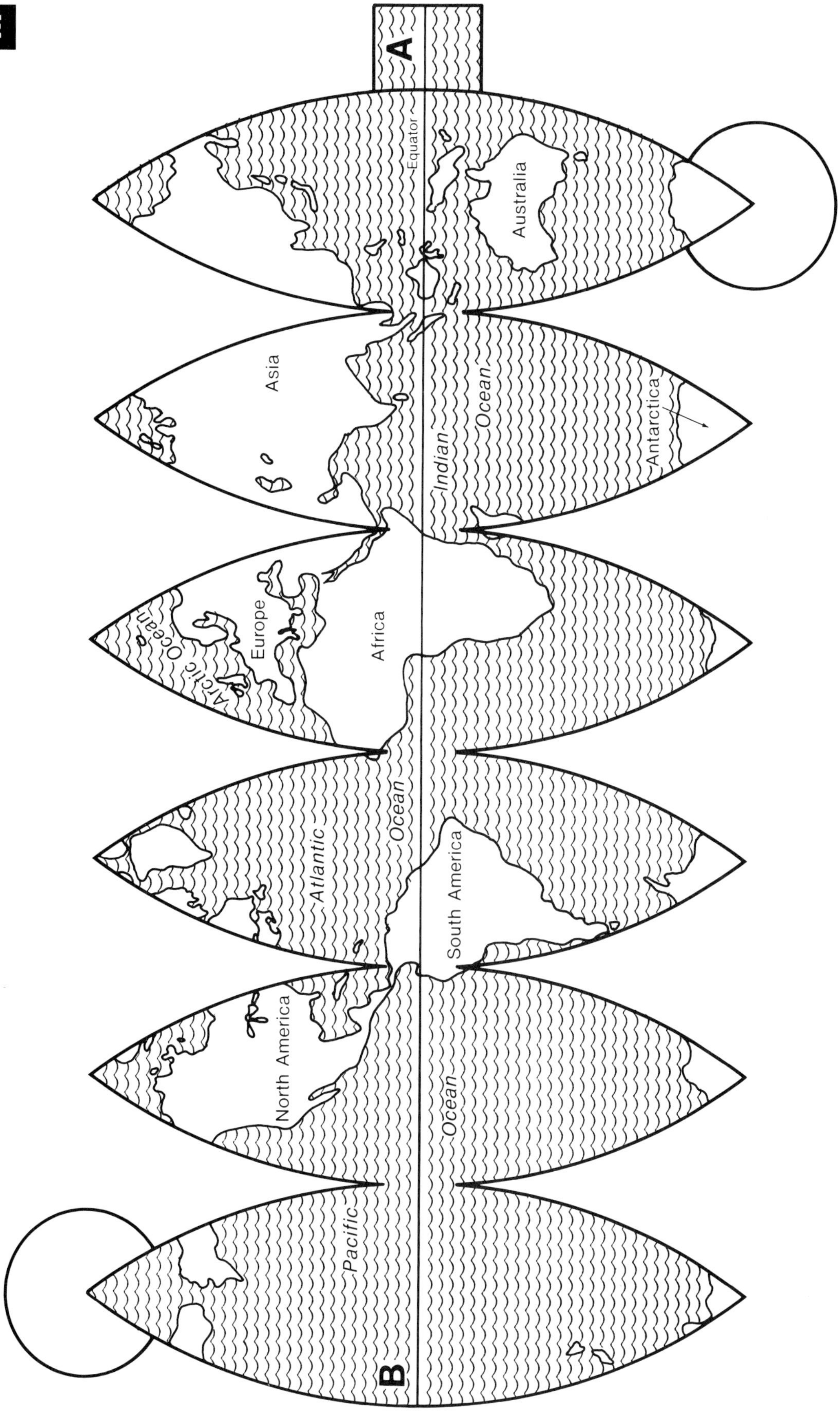

A

Equator

Australia

Asia

Indian Ocean

Antarctica

Arctic Ocean

Europe

Africa

Atlantic Ocean

South America

North America

Pacific Ocean

B

Name _____

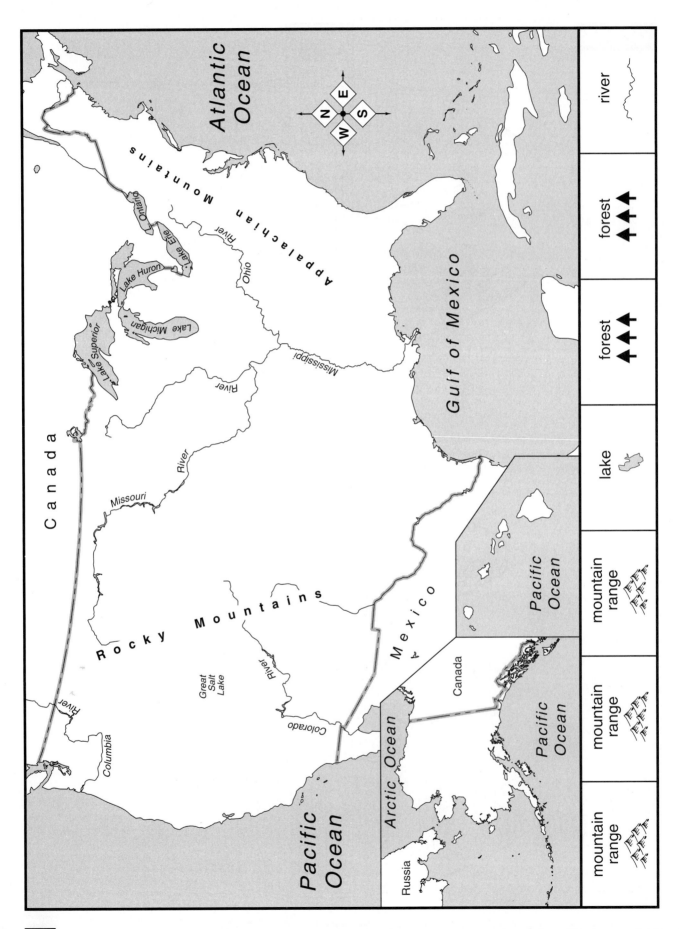

river	
forest	
forest	
lake	
mountain range	
mountain range	
mountain range	

Atlantic Ocean

Appalachian Mountains

Ontario
Lake Erie
Lake Huron
Lake Superior
Lake Michigan

Ohio

Mississippi River

Missouri River

Gulf of Mexico

Canada

Rocky Mountains

Great Salt Lake

River

Colorado

Columbia River

Mexico

Pacific Ocean

Arctic Ocean

Canada

Pacific Ocean

Pacific Ocean

Russia

Name _____

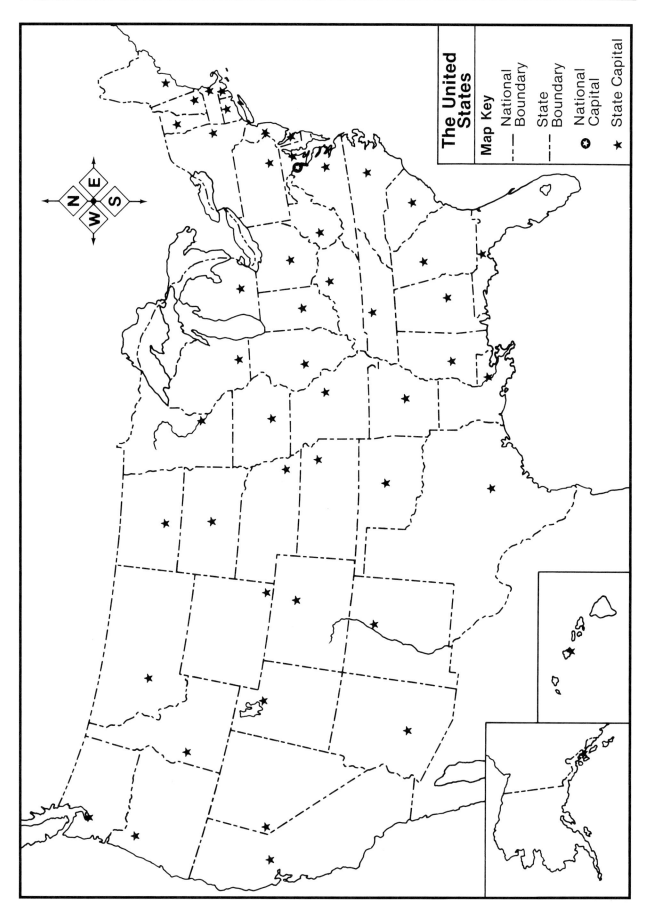

The United States

Map Key

National Boundary — · —

State Boundary — · · —

National Capital ⊛

State Capital ★

Name _____

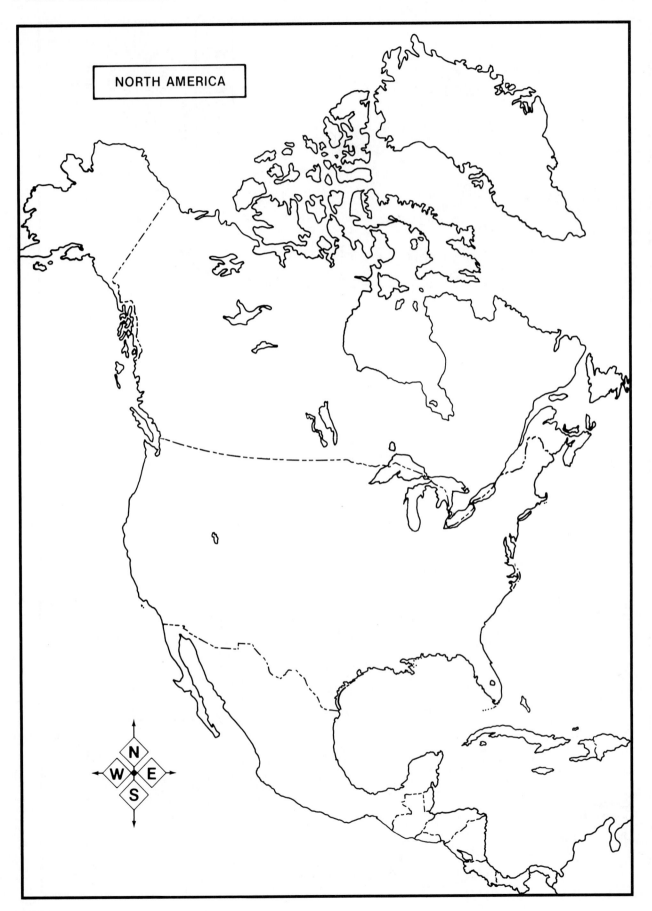

NORTH AMERICA

N
W · E
S

Maps•Globes•Graphs   Level B   © Harcourt Achieve Inc. All rights reserved.

Name _____

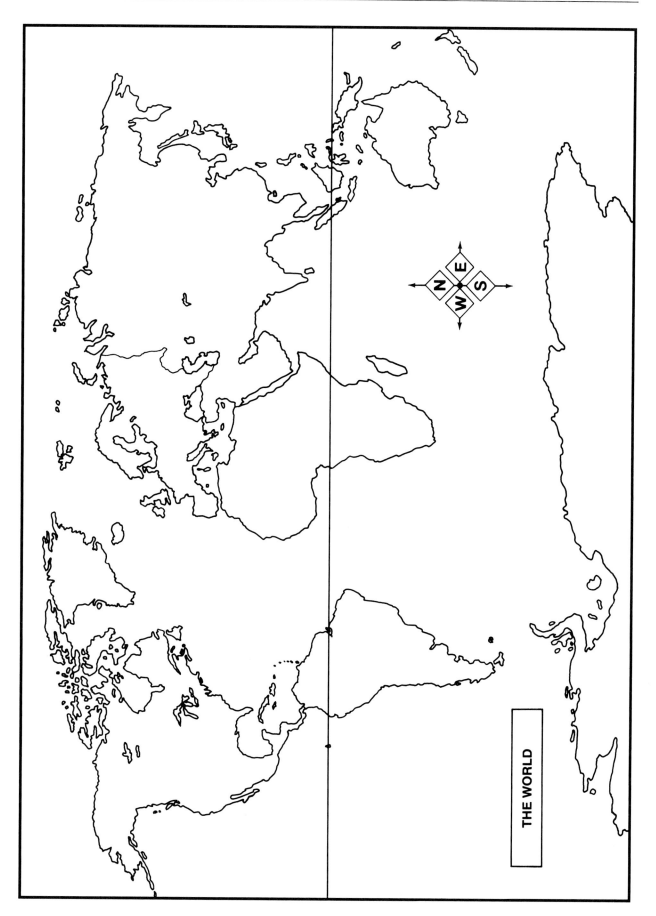

THE WORLD

Name_____

STANDARDIZED TEST

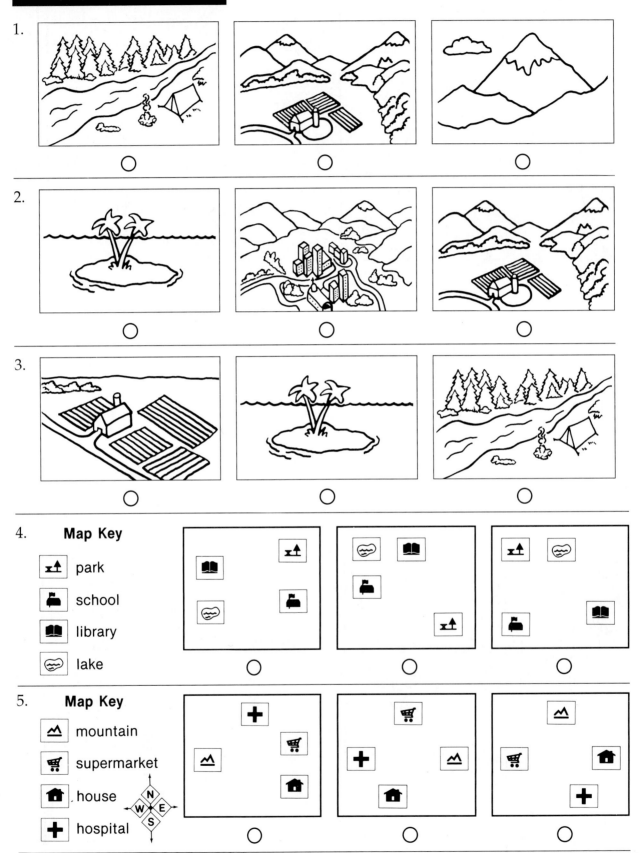

Maps•Globes•Graphs   Level B   © Harcourt Achieve Inc. All rights reserved.

Name _____

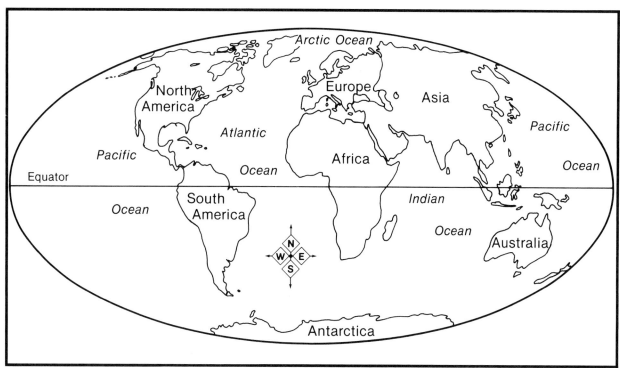

6.
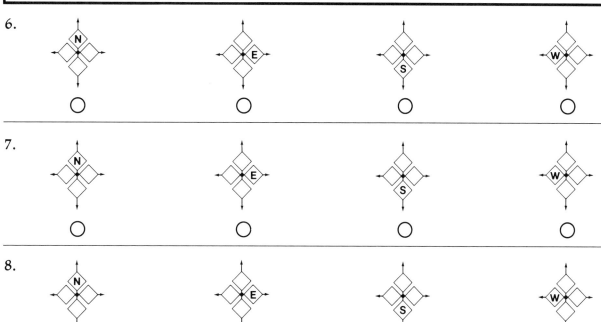

     ◯   ◯   ◯   ◯

7.

     ◯   ◯   ◯   ◯

8.

     ◯   ◯   ◯   ◯

9.

     ◯   ◯   ◯   ◯

Standardized Test Questions
To Be Read by Teacher to Students

Directions for Questions on Page T30

1. Look at the pictures in row 1. Which picture shows a river? Darken the circle under the picture that shows a river.

2. Look at the pictures in row 2. Which picture shows a farm in a valley? Darken the circle under the picture that shows a farm in a valley.

3. Look at the pictures in row 3. Which picture shows an island? Darken the circle under the picture that shows an island.

4. Symbols on a map stand for the real thing. A map key tells what the symbols stand for. Look at the pictures in row 4. The first picture in row 4 shows a map key with the symbols for a park, a school, a library, and a lake. Which one of the pictures shows a park near a lake? Darken the circle for the picture that shows a park near a lake.

5. Look at the pictures in row 5. The first picture shows a map key. It has symbols for a mountain, a supermarket, a house, and a hospital. Which map shows the hospital west of the mountain? Darken the circle for the picture that shows the hospital west of the mountain.

Directions for Questions on Page T31

Look at the map of the world at the top of page T31. Trace the Equator with your finger. Use the map to answer the questions.

6. Look at the compass roses in row 6. They are each marked with a different direction. The first one is marked *N* for north. The second one is marked *E* for east. The third one is marked *S* for south. The last one is marked *W* for west.

Now look at the map of the world. Find Europe on the map. What direction is Europe from Africa? Darken the circle for the compass rose in row 6 that shows the direction Europe is from Africa.

7. Now find North America on the map. What direction is North America from Europe? Darken the circle for the compass rose in row 7 that shows the direction North America is from Europe.

8. Now find the Indian Ocean on the map. What direction is the Indian Ocean from Asia? Darken the circle for the compass rose in row 8 that shows the direction the Indian Ocean is from Asia.

9. Now find Australia. What direction is Australia from the Equator? Darken the circle for the compass rose in row 9 that shows the direction Australia is from the Equator.

Answers appear below.

Page T30	Page T31
1. ● ○ ○	**6.** ● ○ ○ ○
2. ○ ○ ●	**7.** ○ ○ ○ ●
3. ○ ● ○	**8.** ○ ○ ● ○
4. ○ ○ ●	**9.** ○ ○ ● ○
5. ○ ● ○	

Steck Vaughn

Maps
Globes
Graphs

Level B

Writer
Henry Billings

Consultants

Marian Gregory
Teacher
San Luis Coastal Unified School District
San Luis Obispo, California

Gloria Sesso
Supervisor of Social Studies
Half Hollow Hills School District
Dix Hills, New York

Norman McRae, Ph.D.
Former Director of Fine Arts and Social
Studies
Detroit Public Schools
Detroit, Michigan

Edna Whitfield
Former Social Studies Supervisor
St. Louis Public Schools
St. Louis, Missouri

Marilyn Nebenzahl
Social Studies Consultant
San Francisco, California

Karen Wiggins
Director of Social Studies
Richardson Independent School District
Richardson, Texas

Check the Maps•Globes•Graphs Website to find more fun geography activities at home.

Go to www.HarcourtAchieve.com/mggwelcome.html

Harcourt Achieve
Rigby • Steck-Vaughn

www.HarcourtAchieve.com
1.800.531.5015

Acknowledgments

Cartography   Land Registration and Information Service
               Amherst, Nova Scotia, Canada
               Gary J. Robinson
               MapQuest.com, Inc.
               R.R. Donnelley and Sons Company
               XNR Productions Inc., Madison, Wisconsin

Photography Credits

COVER (globe, clouds) © PhotoDisc; p. 4 © Superstock; p. 5(t) © PhotoDisc; p. 5(b) © Corel Photo Studios; pp. 6 (both), 7(t) © PhotoDisc; p. 7(b) © Gale Zucker/Stock Boston; p. 8(t) © Superstock; p. 8(b) © PhotoDisc; p. 9(t) © James Carmichael/The Image Bank; p. 9(b) © PhotoDisc; pp. 16, 22, 30(t) Dale Kirksey; p. 30(b) NASA; p. 36 © PhotoDisc; pp. 44, 52 Gary Russ

Illustration Credits

Dennis Harms pp. 29, 50, 51; David Griffin pp. 14a, 14b, 14c, 14d, 58a, 58b, 58c, 58d, 59; Michael Krone p. 17; T.K. Riddle p. 18; Rusty Kaim p. 4

ISBN 0-7398-9102-2

© 2004 Harcourt Achieve Inc.

Contents

Geography Themes

Geography is the study of Earth and its people. There are five ways to study geography.
- **Location**
- **Place**
- **Human/Environment Interaction**
- **Movement**
- **Regions**

Location tells where something can be found. It tells what is nearby.

Frank lives by a lake. There are trees and mountains near his home.

1. Where is your home? What is it by?

Answers will vary.

2. What is near your home?

Answers will vary, but may include rivers, mountains, cities, farms, and so on.

Place tells what a location is like.

Janis lives in a neighborhood with
  many houses.
She plays in the park on hot
  summer days.

3. How is this place different from where you live?

Answers will vary, but should include physical and human features.

Human/Environment Interaction tells how people
use the land.

Sam lives on a farm.
His family grows corn
  and wheat.

4. How do people use the land where you live?

Answers may include farming, mining, fishing, and ranching.

Human/Environment Interaction tells how people live with the weather. In warm weather people swim. People play baseball. In cold weather people wear hats, coats, and gloves.

There is a lot of rain where Chris lives.

5. What does Chris do in rainy weather?

He wears a raincoat and hat, and he carries an umbrella.

Movement tells how people, goods, and ideas move from place to place.

Manny rides his bicycle to school.
His mother takes a bus to work.

6. How do toys get to the stores?

Answers may include trains, trucks, ships, and airplanes.

Lewis learns new ideas from books.

7. Name other ways ideas move from place to place.

Ideas move through newspapers, magazines, television, radio,

telephones, and computers.

Regions are special areas that share something. Places in a mountain region all have mountains. Regions can be big or small. A neighborhood can be a region.

This picture shows Nathan's neighborhood.

8. How is Nathan's neighborhood like yours?

Students may say that there are houses, apartments, trees, cars, and

a store or market.

1 Land and Water

island

lake

valley

river

An **island** is a piece of land with water all around it.
A **lake** is a body of water with land all around it.
A **river** is a large stream of water that flows into a
larger body of water.
A **valley** is a low place between higher land.

A **hill** is land that rises above the land around it.
A **mountain** is land that rises higher than a hill.
A **plain** is flat land that is good for farming.
An **ocean** is the largest body of water on Earth.

Finding Water and Landforms

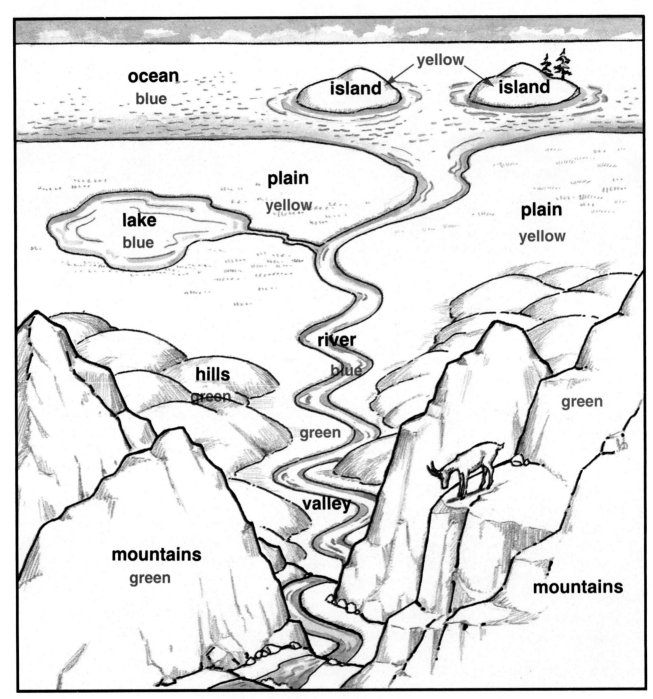

ocean
blue

yellow

island

island

plain
yellow

lake
blue

plain
yellow

hills
green

river
blue

green

green

valley

mountains
green

mountains

1. Read each word on the drawing.

2. Color the bodies of water blue.

3. Color the mountains, hills, and valley green.

4. Color the plains and islands yellow.

Name _____

Finding Water and Landforms

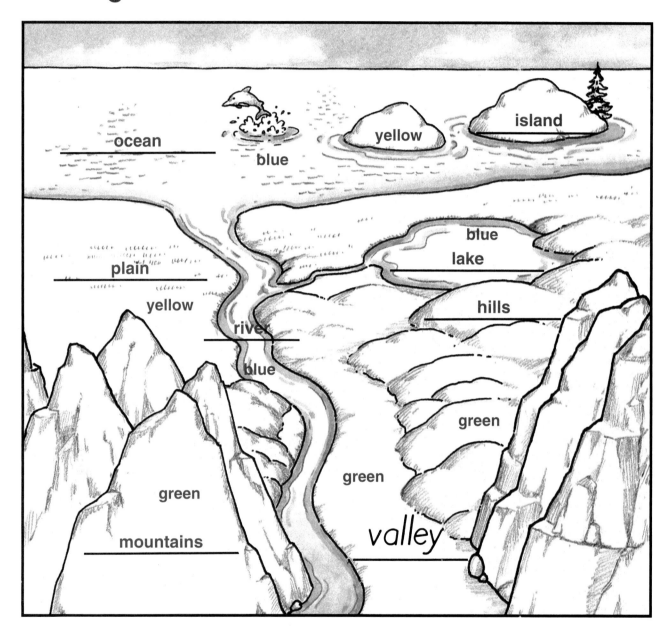

1. Write each word from the list on the line where it belongs.

2. Color the river, lake, and ocean blue.

3. Color the mountains, hills, and valley green.

4. Color the plain and islands yellow.

Finding Water and Landforms

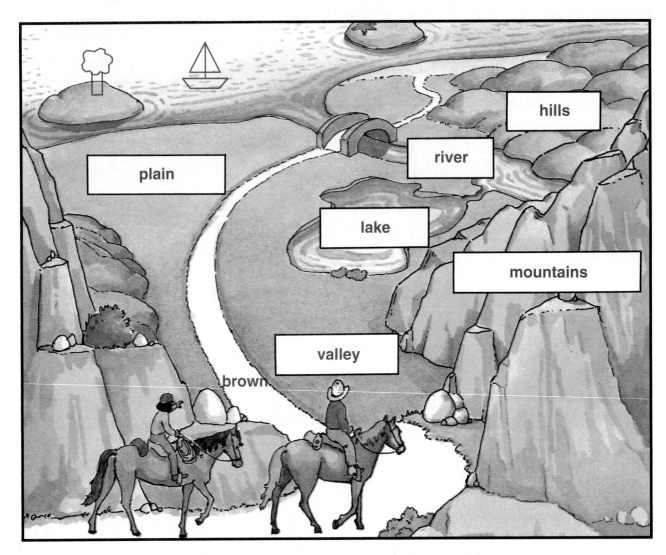

Imagine you and your friend are riding horses. You ride down the trail to the beach.

1. Find the trail. Color it brown.
2. Write the name of each place you pass in the box where it belongs.

   mountains   lake   river
   valley   hills   plain

3. Draw a boat on the ocean.
4. Draw a tree on an island.

Name _____

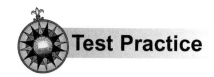

Skill Check

Words I Know   island   plain   hill   mountain
              ocean   river   lake   valley

1. What is land that is higher than a hill? ___a mountain___

2. What is water with land all around it? ___a lake___

3. Draw a line to match each word with its picture.

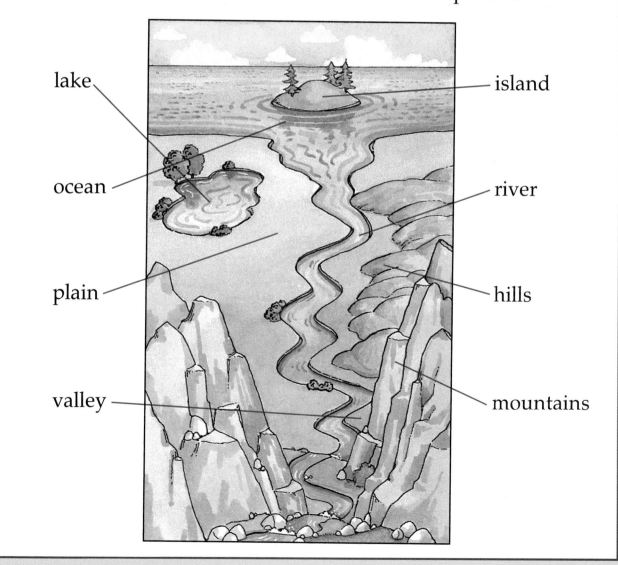

lake

ocean

plain

valley

island

river

hills

mountains

Geography Themes Up Close

Human/Environment Interaction tells how people live, work, and play on Earth. Look at the pictures. They show people in different places. People do different things during the year. They make changes when it is hot or when it is cold. They change what they do. They change what they wear. Write what the people are doing below each picture.

1.

playing in the snow in winter

3.

playing outside in summer

2.

wearing special clothes to keep dry in the rain

4.

wearing warm clothes in winter

People make changes to the land. In each box below, draw a picture showing how people change the land.

5. People build houses.

7. People build roads.

6. People plant gardens.

8. Draw a change in your neighborhood.

 **Maps and Map Keys**

This **photo** shows a small town.

It was taken from above.

▶ What things can you see in the photo?

Name _____

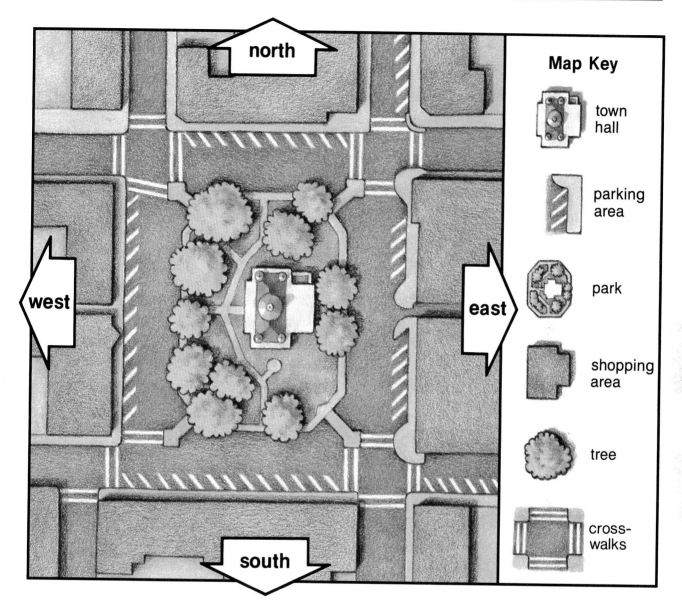

This map shows the same town.
A **map** is a drawing of a real place.
Symbols on the map stand for real things.
The **map key** tells what the symbols stand for.

Study the map key. Count the symbols on the map.
How many of each symbol are on the map? **Answers may vary, depending on student's interpretation.**

town halls ___1___   parks ___1___   shopping areas ___10___

parking areas ___7___   trees ___11___   cross-walks ___4___

Reading Symbols on a Map

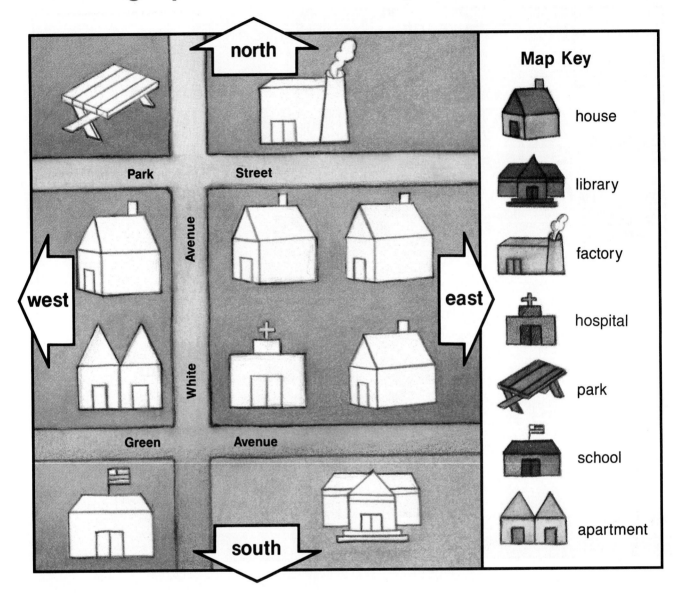

This map shows a neighborhood.

1. Circle each thing below that is closer to the school than to the park.

    (hospital)   (apartment)   (library)   factory

2. How many houses are there? _____4_____

3. How many streets? _____3_____

4. Color the symbols on the map to match the map key. **colors similar to key**

Name _____

Reading Symbols on a Map

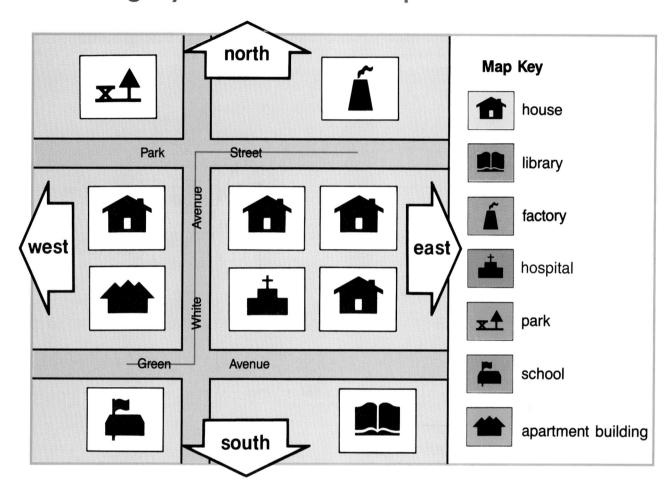

This map shows the same neighborhood.

1. Draw a red line showing how to get from the factory to the school.

2. What streets will you take? _____

   _____ Park Street, White Avenue, Green Avenue _____

3. Name three things you pass. _____ house _____

   _____ apartment _____   _____ hospital _____

4. Color the map to match the map key. colors similar to key

Finding Symbols on a Map

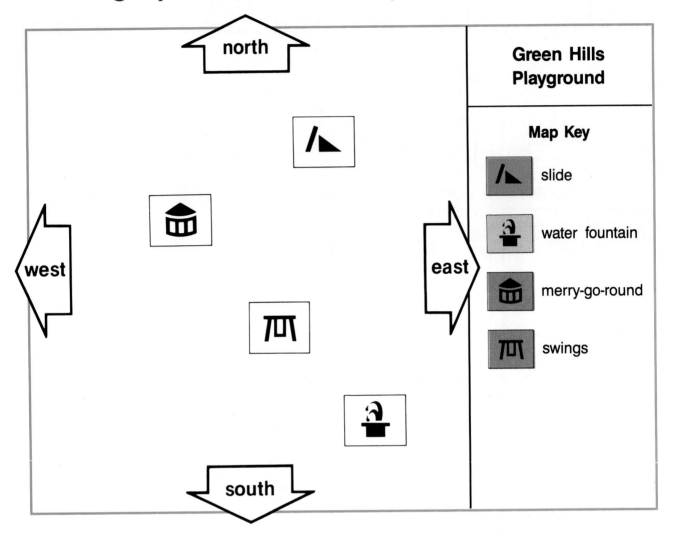

1. What is the name of this playground?

   Green Hills Playground

2. Circle the answers.

   The slide is nearest the

   (merry-go-round.)   water fountain.

   The swings are farthest from the

   (slide.)   water fountain.

3. Draw a water fountain next to the slide. **Placement will vary, but the water fountain should be drawn close to the slide.**

4. Color the map to match the map key. **colors similar to key**

Name _____

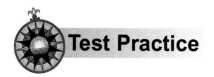

Skill Check

Words I Know   **map**   **symbol**   **map key**   **photo**

Write the correct word next to each picture.

s <u>y</u> <u>m</u> <u>b</u> <u>o</u> <u>l</u>   m <u>a</u> <u>p</u> k <u>e</u> <u>y</u>

Finding Symbols on a Map

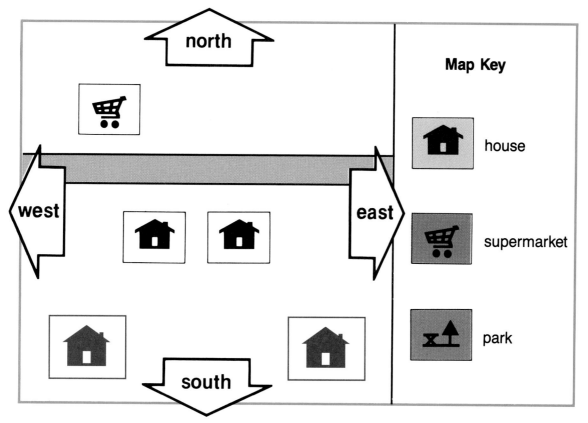

1. Draw a park next to the supermarket. **Placement will vary, but the park should be drawn close to the supermarket.**

2. Draw two houses at the bottom of the map.

3. Color the map to match the map key. **colors similar to key**

North, south, east, and west are four **directions**.
The boy is facing north. If the boy knows one direction,
he can figure out all the other directions.

Here is how you can do it:

South is opposite north.
When north is in front, south is behind you.
When north is in front, east is to your right.
West is opposite east. So west is to your left.

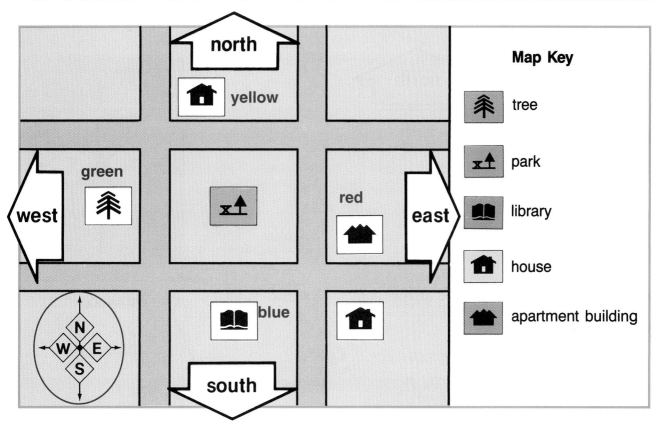

A **compass rose** is a symbol that shows direction.
It looks like this ⬖. Find it on the map.

The letters <u>N</u>, <u>S</u>, <u>E</u>, and <u>W</u> stand for north, south, east, and west. Find the letters on the compass rose.

1. Circle the compass rose on the map.

2. Name the opposite of each direction.

north _____ south _____   east _____ west _____

south _____ north _____   west _____ east _____

3. Color the house on the north yellow.

4. Color the library on the south blue.

5. Color the apartment on the east red.

6. Color the tree on the west green.

Finding Directions on a Map

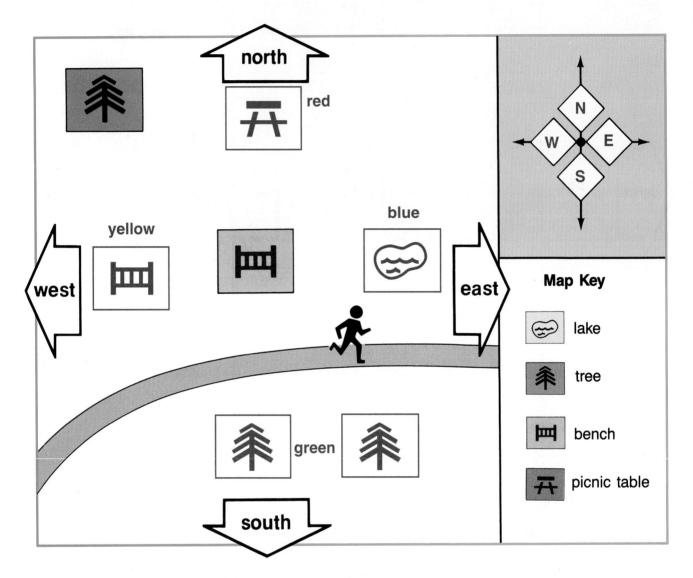

North is at the top of this map of a park.

1. Write the letters <u>N</u>, <u>S</u>, <u>E</u>, and <u>W</u> where they belong on the compass rose.

2. Draw a picnic table on the north. Color it red.

3. Draw a lake on the east. Color it blue.

4. Draw two trees on the south. Color them green.

5. Draw a bench on the west. Color it yellow.

6. In which direction is the person running? _____east_____

Name _____

Finding Directions on a Map

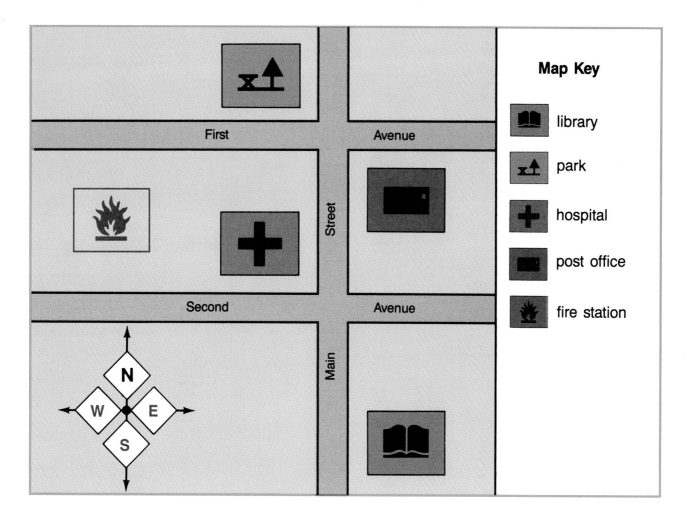

1. Write <u>S</u>, <u>E</u>, and <u>W</u> on the compass rose.
2. Write the direction that completes each sentence.

   The park is _____north_____ of the hospital.

   The post office is _____east_____ of the hospital.

   The library is _____south_____ of the post office.

   The hospital is _____west_____ of the post office.
3. Draw a fire station west of the hospital.

Finding Directions on a Map

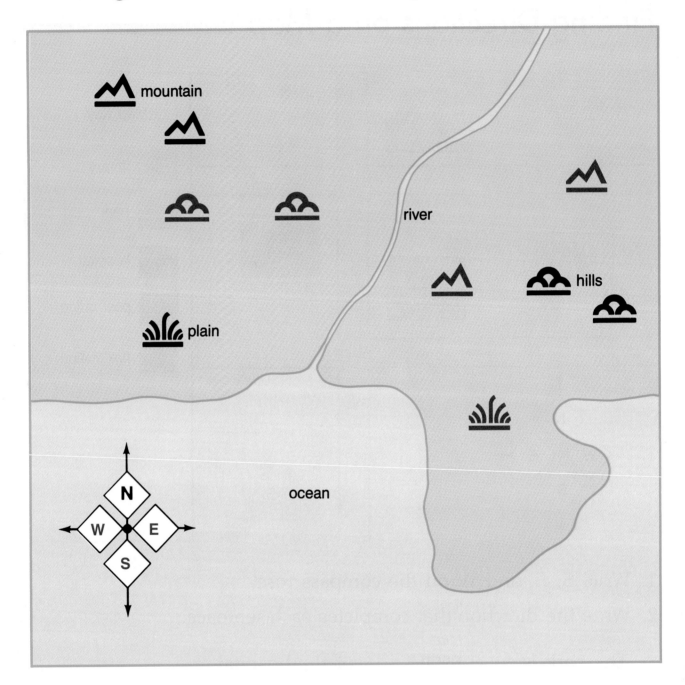

1. Write <u>S</u>, <u>E</u>, and <u>W</u> on the compass rose.
2. Draw a mountain east of the river. Use .
3. Draw a plain south of the hills. Use .
4. Draw a mountain north of the hills. Use .
5. Draw two hills west of the river. Use .

Name _____

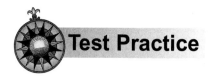

Skill Check

Words I Know   **directions**   **north**   **east**
                      compass rose   **south**   **west**

1. Which direction is opposite east? _____ west _____

2. Which direction is opposite north? _____ south _____

3. What is this symbol? ⬧ _____ compass rose _____

Finding Directions on a Map

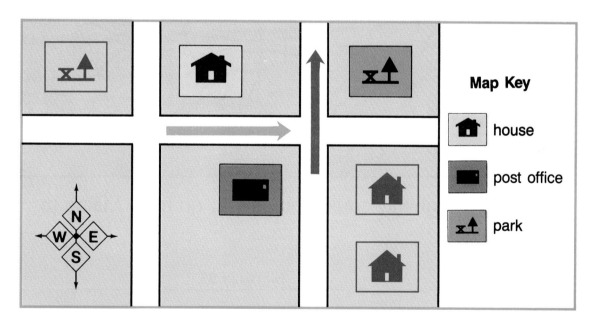

1. Draw a park west of the house.

2. Draw two houses east of the post office.

3. In which direction is the blue arrow pointing? ___ east ___

4. In which direction is the red arrow pointing? ___ north ___

Geography Themes Up Close

Movement means how people, goods, and ideas get from one place to another. Highways move people and goods from place to place.

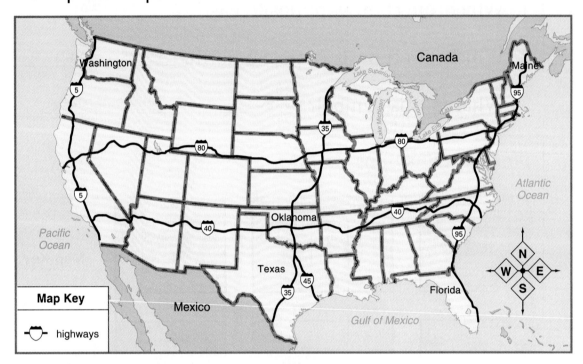

1. What highway could you take to go from Maine to Florida?

   Highway 95

2. What highways could a truck use to take apples from Washington to Oklahoma?

   Highways 5 and 40

3. What three highways go through Texas?

   Highways 40, 35, and 45

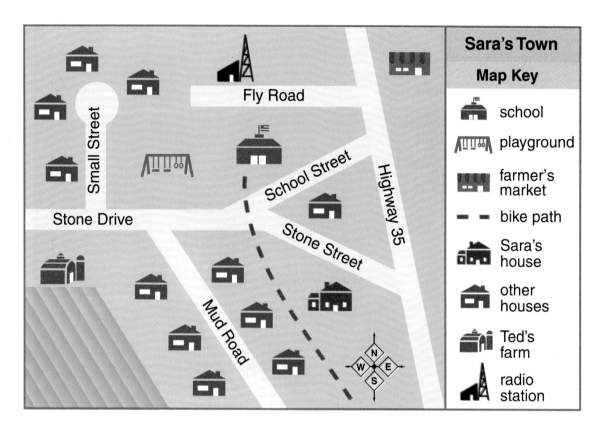

4. How can Sara get to school?

ride her bike on the bike path, walk, take a bus, or ride in a car down
Stone Street to School Street

**5. Ted grows corn on his farm. What streets and highways
can he use to get his corn to the farmer's market?**

Stone Drive, School Street, Highway 35

Ideas also move from place to place in Sara's town.
Television is one way ideas move from place to place.

6. What are other ways that ideas move in Sara's town?

radio, telephone, computers, books, newspapers, magazines

4 Globes

The small photo shows Earth.
It was taken from out in space.

The large photo shows a **globe**. A globe is a model of
Earth. It is round like Earth.

Blue always stands for water. The oceans are the largest
bodies of water. On this globe green stands for land. On
other globes land can be other colors. **Continents** are the
largest landforms.

▶ Find the globe in your classroom. What color is the land?

Name _____

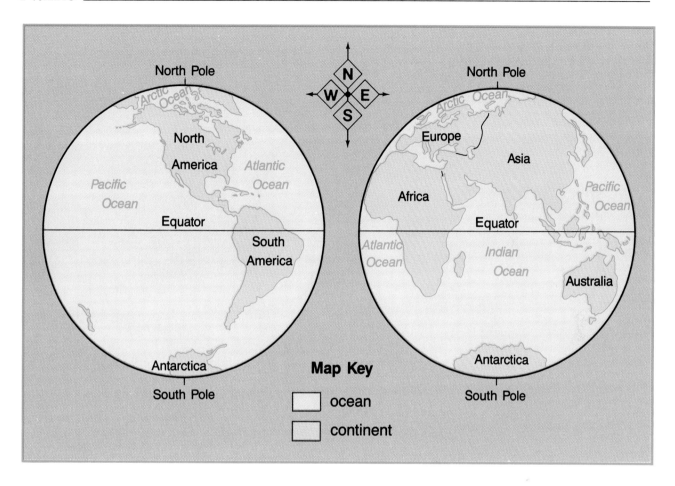

The globe is round like a ball. You can't see the whole thing at once. Here are both sides of one globe. Count the seven continents and four oceans. Earth is mostly covered by water.

The Seven Continents

North America	Australia	Europe	Antarctica
South America	Africa	Asia	

The Four Oceans

Pacific Ocean	Indian Ocean
Atlantic Ocean	Arctic Ocean

Can you see the line drawn around the center of the globe? This line is the **Equator**. It is an imaginary line that divides Earth in half.

Finding Directions on a Globe

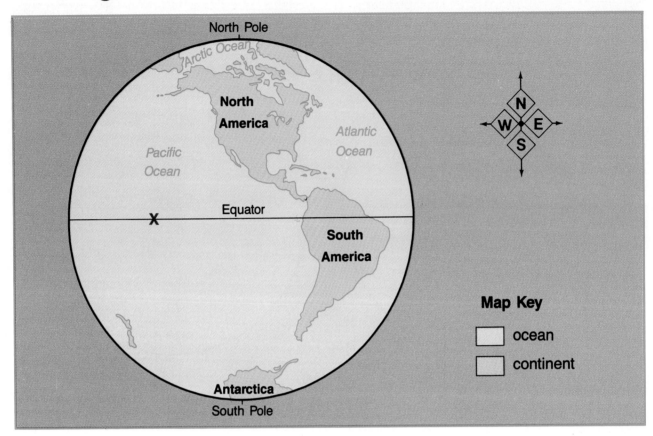

1. Find the Equator. Put an **X** on it.

2. Which continent is north of the Equator?

   North America

3. Which continent does the Equator pass through?

   South America

4. Which ocean is east of the two continents?

   Atlantic Ocean

5. Which ocean is west of the two continents?

   Pacific Ocean

Name _____

Mapping a Globe

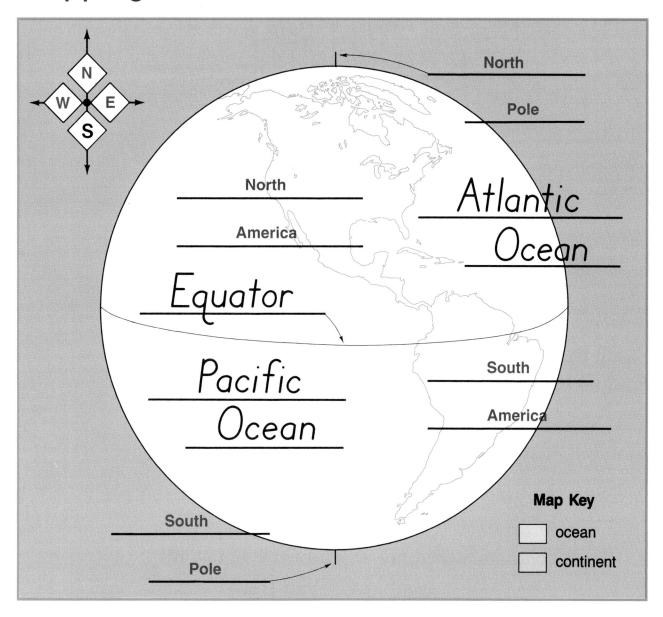

1. Complete the compass rose.

2. Write these names on the globe where they belong.

    North America   South Pole

    South America   North Pole

3. Color the continents to match the map key. colors similar to key

4. Color the oceans to match the map key.

Finding Directions on Globes

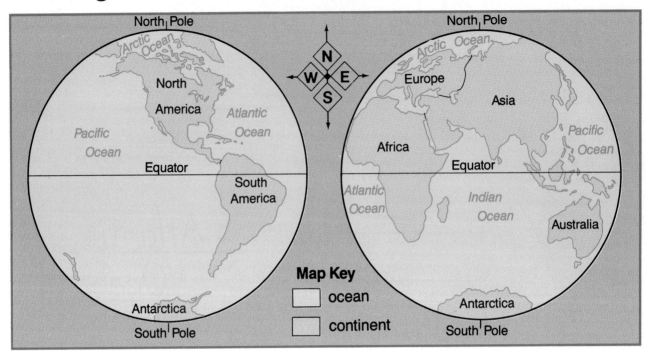

Map Key
☐ ocean
☐ continent

Study the map.
Find all seven continents. Find the four oceans.

1. Which continents are only north of the Equator?

   <u>North America</u>   <u>Europe</u>

   <u>Asia</u>

2. Which continents are only south of the Equator?

   <u>Australia</u>   <u>Antarctica</u>

3. Which continents are north <u>and</u> south of the Equator?

   <u>Africa</u>   <u>South America</u>

4. Which ocean is east of Africa? <u>Indian Ocean</u>

5. Which ocean is west of North America? <u>Pacific Ocean</u>

Name _____

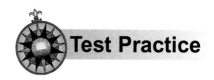

Skill Check

Words I Know   **globe**   **continent**   **ocean**

Write the correct word next to each picture.

   _____globe_____

   _____continent_____

Mapping a Globe

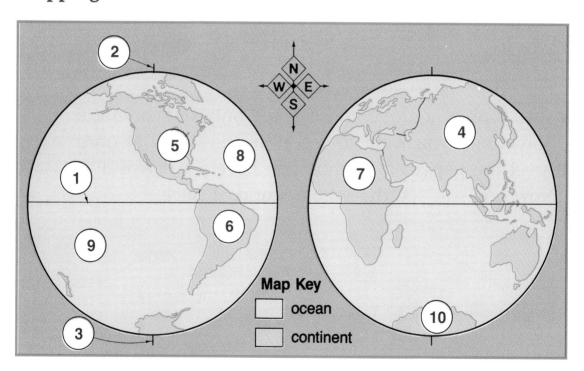

Write the number of each place on the map where it belongs.

① Equator   ⑤ North America   ⑨ Pacific Ocean
② North Pole   ⑥ South America   ⑩ Antarctica
③ South Pole   ⑦ Africa
④ Asia   ⑧ Atlantic Ocean

When you look at a globe you can see only one side at a time. Sometimes you want to see all of the world at once. If you peel the paper off a globe you have a flat world map. Now you can see the whole world at once.

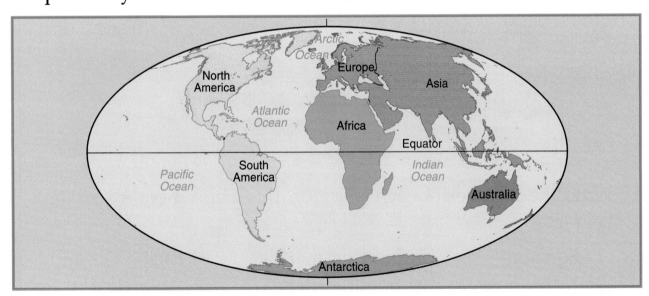

What continents can you see on this map that you can't see on the globes? What ocean can you see on this map that you can't see on the globes? How else are they different?

Name _____

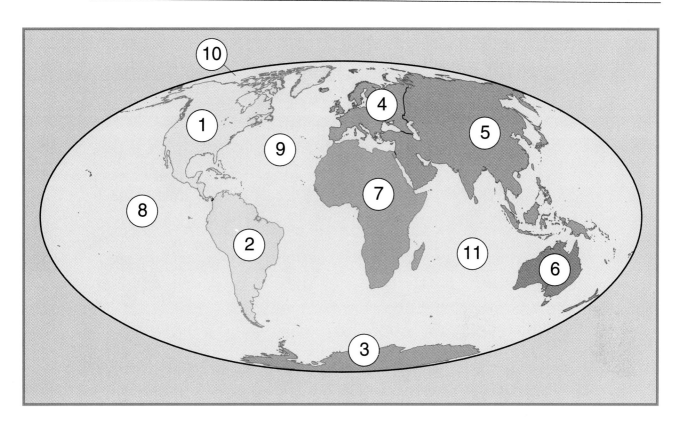

This map shows all seven continents and four oceans.

Write the continent and ocean names on these lines.

Continents

① _____ **North America** _____

② _____ **South America** _____

③ _____ **Antarctica** _____

④ _____ **Europe** _____

⑤ _____ **Asia** _____

⑥ _____ **Australia** _____

⑦ _____ **Africa** _____

Oceans

⑧ _____ **Pacific Ocean** _____

⑨ _____ **Atlantic Ocean** _____

⑩ _____ **Arctic Ocean** _____

⑪ _____ **Indian Ocean** _____

Finding Continents and Oceans

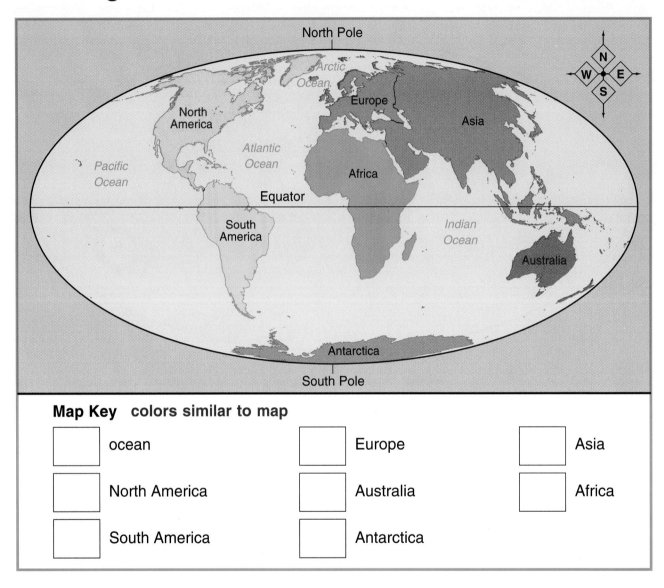

Map Key   colors similar to map

☐ ocean

☐ North America

☐ South America

☐ Europe

☐ Australia

☐ Antarctica

☐ Asia

☐ Africa

This map shows the world's continents and oceans.

1. Color the map key to match the map.

2. Name two continents west of the Atlantic Ocean.

   <u>**North America**</u>   <u>**South America**</u>

3. Name two continents south of Europe.

   **Answers will vary but should include two of the following:
   Asia, Africa, Antarctica, South America, Australia**

Name _____

Finding Continents and Oceans

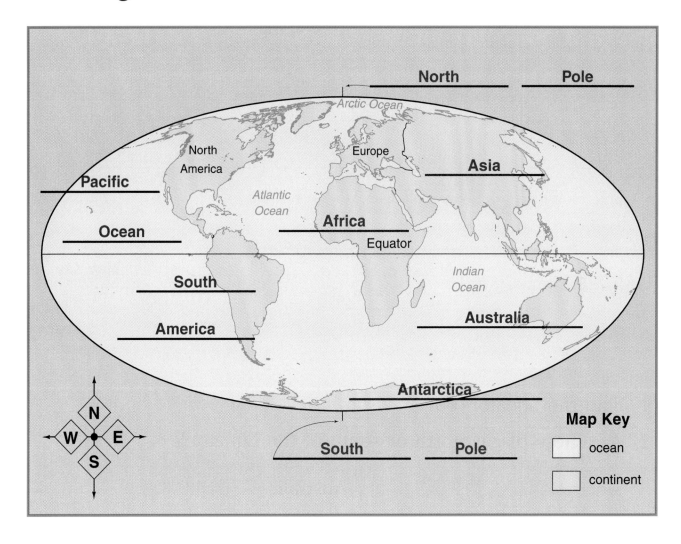

1. Write these names on the map where they belong.

   South America   Australia   North Pole
   Asia   Antarctica   South Pole
   Africa   Pacific Ocean

2. Name two continents that touch the Indian Ocean.

   **Answers will vary but should include two of the following:
   Asia, Africa, Australia, Antarctica**

   _____   _____

3. Name two continents that touch the Atlantic Ocean.

   **Answers will vary but should include two of the following:
   North America, South America, Europe, Africa, Antarctica.**

   _____   _____

Finding Directions on a World Map

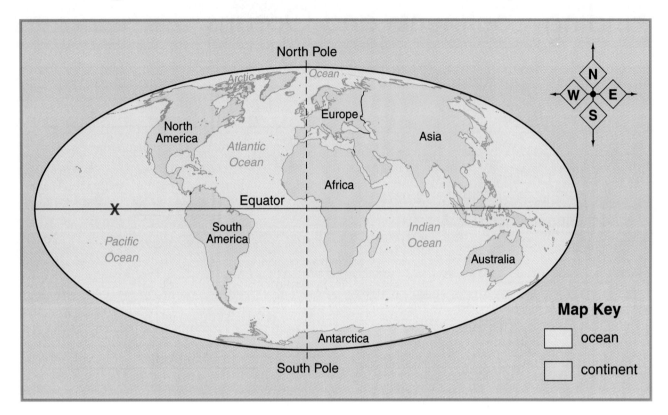

1. Find the Equator. Put an **X** on it.
2. Are these places <u>north</u> or <u>south</u> of the Equator?

   Antarctica ___south___   Australia ___south___

   North America ___north___   Europe ___north___

   Arctic Ocean ___north___   Asia ___north___

3. Finish the line between the North and South Poles.
4. Are these places <u>east</u> or <u>west</u> of the line you drew?

   South America ___west___   Asia ___east___

   Australia ___east___   Indian Ocean ___east___

   North America ___west___   Atlantic Ocean <u>west and east</u>

Name _____

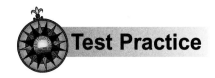

Skill Check

Finding Places on a Map

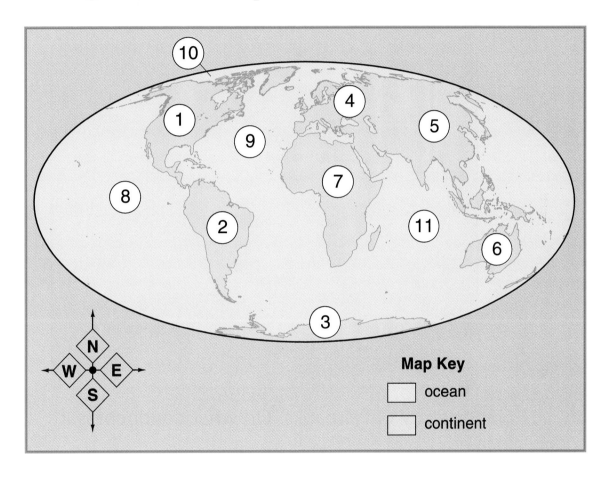

Map Key

☐ ocean

☐ continent

Each place is numbered on the map. Write each number from the map next to its name below.

__1__ North America   __6__ Australia   __7__ Africa

__2__ South America   __3__ Antarctica   __4__ Europe

__9__ Atlantic Ocean   __11__ Indian Ocean   __5__ Asia

__8__ Pacific Ocean   __10__ Arctic Ocean

Geography Themes Up Close

Location tells where something is found. Every place on Earth has a location.

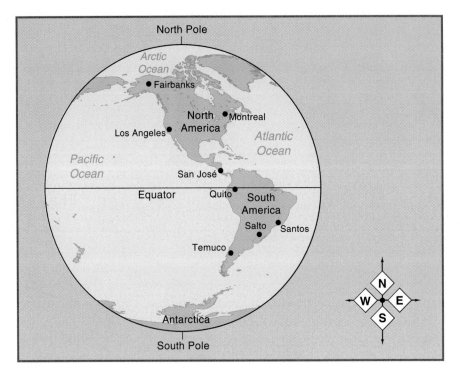

1. Find the city of Fairbanks. On what continent is it located?

   North America

2. Is Fairbanks north or south of the Equator?

   North

3. This city is in South America. It is very near the Equator. Name the city.

   Quito

A **grid** is made of lines that cross to make squares. A grid on a map helps you find a place. Look at the grid on the world map below.

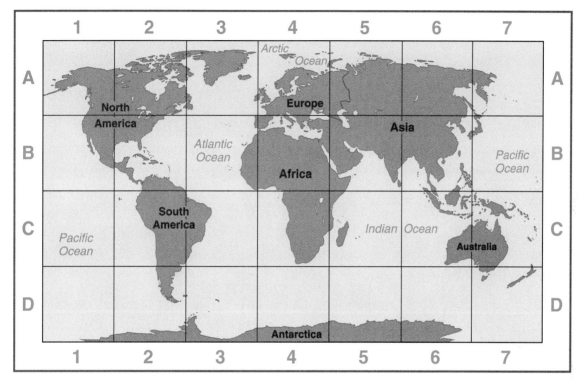

4. What continent is in square B-1?

_____ **North America** _____

5. What ocean is in square A-4?

_____ **Arctic Ocean** _____

6. What continent is in square C-7?

_____ **Australia** _____

7. What ocean is in C-5 and C-6?

_____ **Indian Ocean** _____

6 Boundaries

Can you see North America on this globe? North America has three large countries. They are Canada, Mexico, and the United States.

Can you see the edges or lines around each country? These are called **boundaries**. Boundaries show the end of one place and the beginning of another.

Name _____

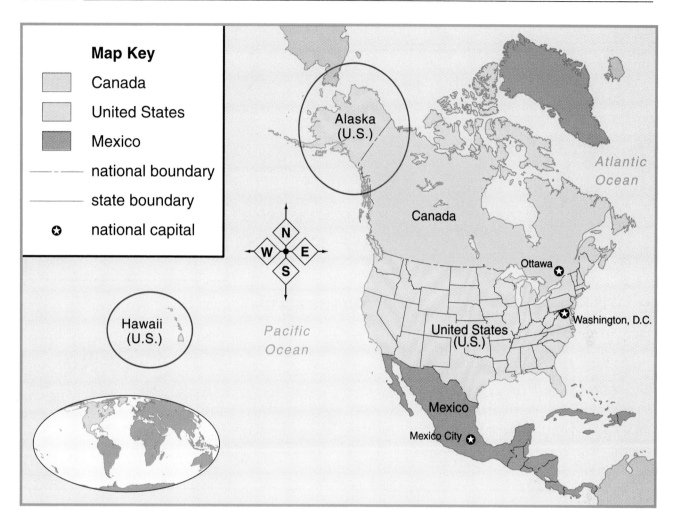

The small map shows where North America is in the world. The large map shows North America by itself.

Find the United States on the map. It is divided into 50 different states. A **state boundary** is shown with a solid black line. Alaska and Hawaii are states that are away from the rest of the United States. Find Alaska and Hawaii on the map. Circle them.

Canada is the country north of the United States. Mexico is the country south of the United States. Each country, or nation, has one capital city. The map key shows the symbols for a **national boundary** and a **national capital**. Circle one example of each symbol on the map.

Finding Places in North America

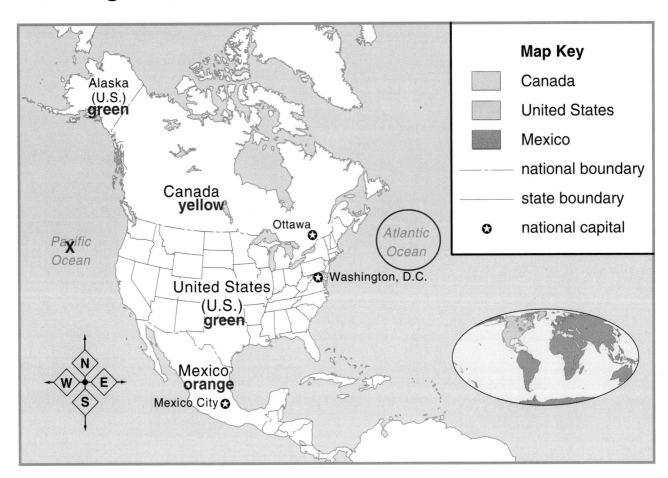

1. Color the United States green. Alaska and Hawaii are part of the U.S. Hawaii is not part of North America.

2. Color Canada yellow.

3. Color Mexico orange.

4. What is the capital of Mexico? _____ Mexico City _____

5. What is the capital of Canada? _____ Ottawa _____

6. What is the capital of the U.S.? _____ Washington, D.C. _____

7. Circle the ocean name that is east of North America.

8. Put an **X** on the ocean name that is west of North America.

Name _____

Finding Places in North America

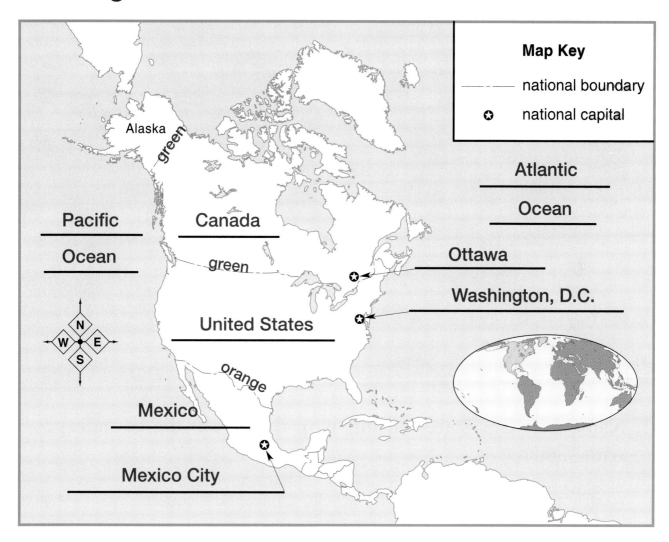

1. Write these names on the map where they belong.
   Atlantic Ocean   Mexico   United States
   Pacific Ocean   Canada   Washington, D.C.
   Mexico City   Ottawa

2. Draw a green line to show the boundaries between
   the U.S. and Canada. Remember that Alaska
   is part of the U.S.

3. Draw an orange line to show the boundary between
   the U.S. and Mexico.

Finding Boundaries

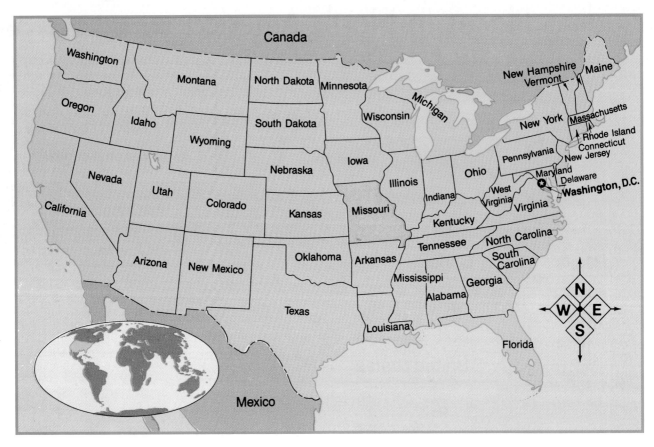

1. Name four U.S. states on this map that touch the boundary with Canada.

   Answers will vary but should include four of the following:
   Washington, Idaho, Montana, North Dakota, Minnesota, Michigan,
   New York, Vermont, New Hampshire, Maine.

   _____   _____

2. Name two states that touch the boundary with Mexico.

   Answers will vary but should include two of the following:
   California, Arizona, New Mexico, Texas.

3. Name one state that touches each side of Missouri.

   north _____**Iowa**_____   east _____**Illinois, Kentucky, or Tennesseee**_____

   south _____**Arkansas**_____   west _____**Nebraska, Kansas, or Oklahoma**_____

Name _____

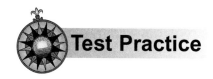

Skill Check

Words I Know **boundary** **state boundary**
national boundary **national capital**

Draw the symbols for:

— — —	——————	⭐
national boundary	state boundary	national capital

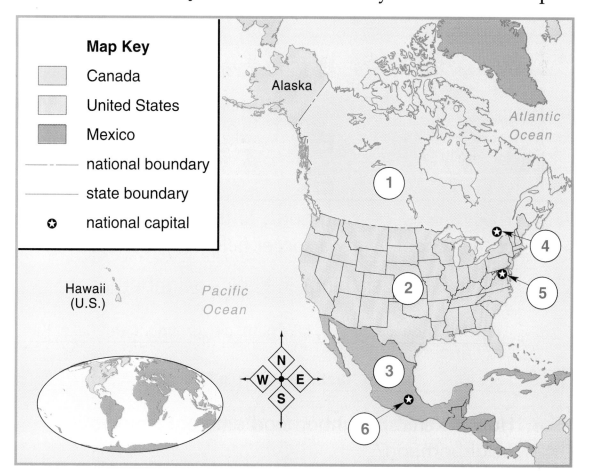

Map Key

Canada

United States

Mexico

— · — · — national boundary

——— state boundary

✪ national capital

Alaska

Atlantic Ocean

Hawaii (U.S.)

Pacific Ocean

① ② ③ ④ ⑤ ⑥

N W E S

Write the number of each place on the map where it belongs.

① Canada   ③ Mexico   ⑤ Washington, D.C.
② United States   ④ Ottawa   ⑥ Mexico City

Place tells what a location is like. It tells what makes a location special.

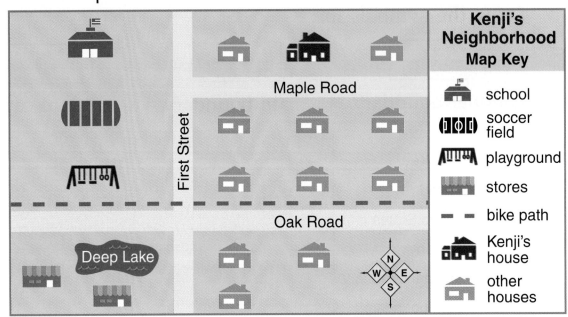

1. There is a soccer field north of the playground. It is south of the school. Draw a soccer field on the map.

2. Name two other things in Kenji's neighborhood.

   Any two: houses, stores, bike path, playground, Deep Lake, Kenji's

   house, First Street, Maple Road, Oak Road

3. How is Kenji's neighborhood different from your neighborhood?

   Answers will vary. Accept all reasonable answers.

Place has things from nature like trees and rivers. Place also has things like houses that people build.

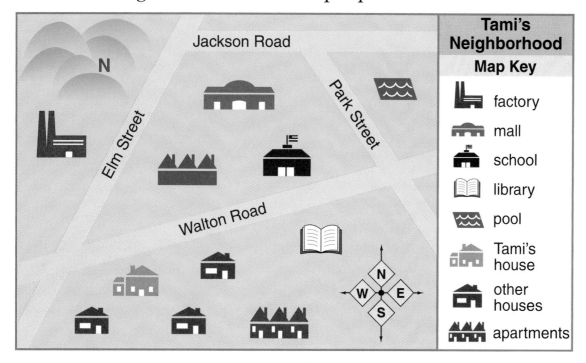

4. There are apartments south of the mall. Draw the apartments on the map.

5. The pool is east of the mall. Is the pool from nature or did people build it?

   People built it.
   _____

6. Find the hills on the map. Mark an **N** on them if they are from nature. Mark a **P** if people made them.

7. What things in the neighborhood did people build?

   houses, apartments, school, library, pool, mall, factory
   _____

   _____

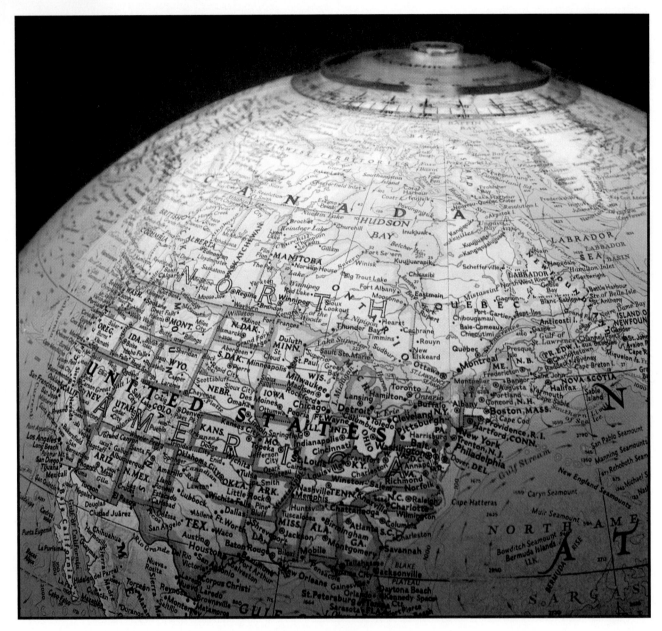

The words on a globe are called **labels**. The labels name the places on the globe.

Continents and oceans are the largest places. They have the biggest labels. Find the label for North America.

Countries, states, cities, and lakes are smaller places. They have smaller labels. Find the labels for United States, Canada, Ohio, Washington, D.C., and Lake Superior on the globe.

Name _____

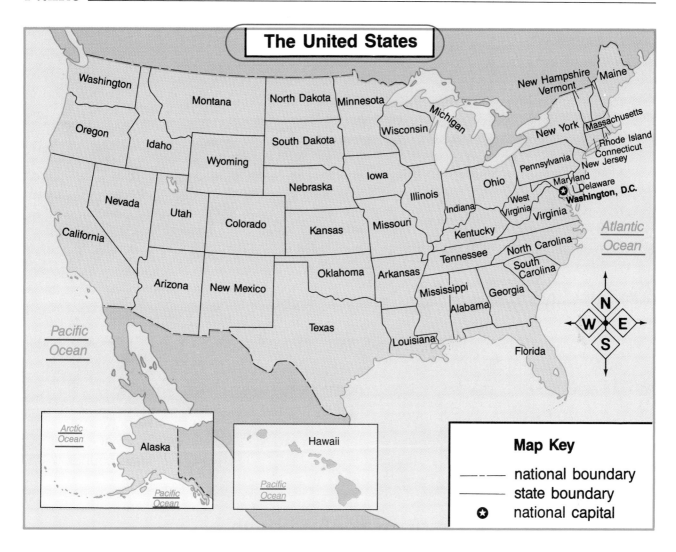

This map has a **title** or name. The title tells you what you are looking at. The title has the biggest, darkest letters on the map.

Alaska and Hawaii are far away from the other 48 states. They appear in special boxes called **inset maps**. Now you can see all 50 states on one page.

1. Circle one inset map. **Either the inset map of Alaska or the inset map of Hawaii should be circled.**

2. Circle the map title.

3. Draw a box around your state's label. **Teacher will have to determine correct answer.**

4. Draw a line under the ocean labels.

Reading Map Labels

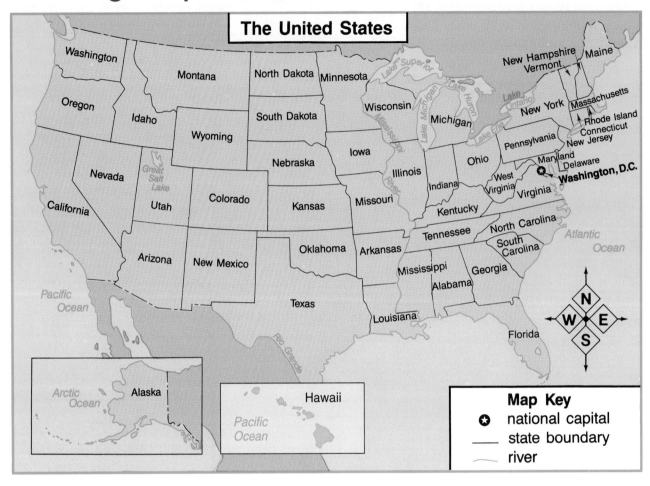

Find the river that goes from north to south.
It is the Mississippi River.
The Mississippi River is a boundary for many states.

1. Name six states with a boundary formed by a river.

   Answers will vary but should include six of the following:

   Minnesota, Iowa, Missouri, Arkansas, Louisiana, Wisconsin,

   Illinois, Kentucky, Tennessee, Mississippi, Texas.

2. What is the title of the map? _____ The United States

Name _____

Finding Places in the United States

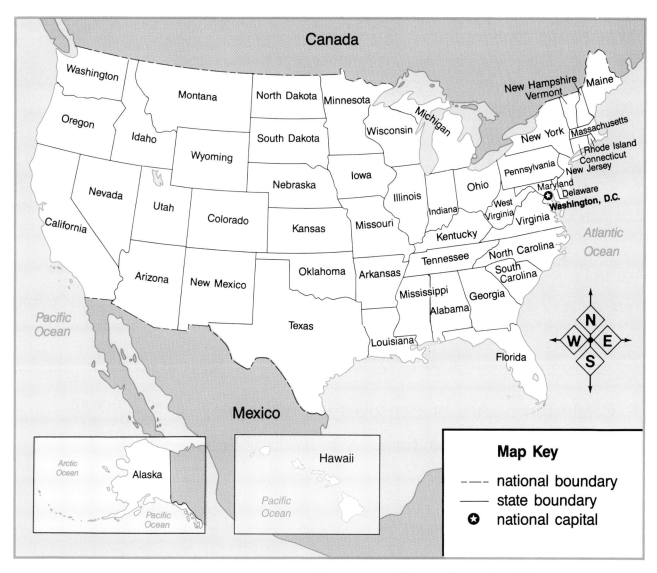

1. Make up a title for the map. Answers will vary but should include "United States."

2. Find your state on the map. Circle it. Answers will vary.

3. Find two countries outside the U.S. Name them.

_____ Canada _____   _____ Mexico _____

4. Color the states touching Canada yellow.
   Color the states touching Mexico brown.   **Color to match the directions**

Finding Water and Landforms

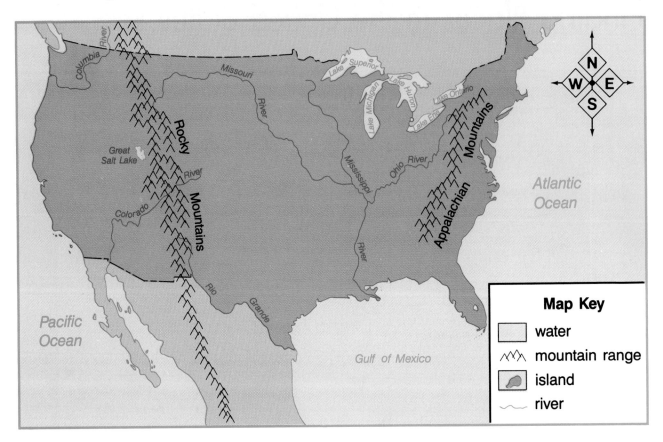

1. Circle the names of two oceans on the map. **Atlantic Ocean, Pacific Ocean**

2. Name the river that forms a boundary between two countries.

   <u>   **Rio Grande**   </u>

3. Name three other rivers. _____

   Answers will vary but should include three of the following:
   Mississippi, Colorado, Missouri, Ohio, Columbia.

4. Name two lakes. _____

   Answers will vary but should include two of the following: Lake Superior,
   Lake Michigan, Lake Huron, Lake Ontario, Lake Erie, Great Salt Lake.

5. Circle one mountain range on the map. **Either the Rocky Mountains or the Appalachian Mountains should be circled.**

Name _____

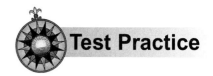

Skill Check

Words I Know   **label   title   inset map**

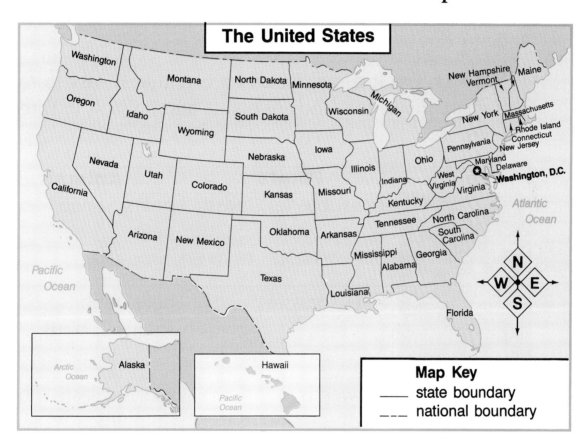

The United States

Washington
Montana
North Dakota   Minnesota
Oregon
Idaho
Wyoming
South Dakota
Wisconsin
Michigan
New Hampshire   Maine
Vermont
New York   Massachusetts
Rhode Island
Connecticut
Pennsylvania   New Jersey
Nevada
Utah
Colorado
Nebraska
Iowa
Illinois
Indiana
Ohio
Maryland
Delaware
West Virginia   Washington, D.C.
California
Kansas
Missouri
Virginia
Kentucky
Atlantic Ocean
Arizona   New Mexico
Oklahoma   Arkansas
Tennessee   North Carolina
South Carolina
Mississippi   Georgia
Alabama
Pacific Ocean
Texas
Louisiana
Florida

N
W   E
S

Arctic Ocean   Alaska
Hawaii
Pacific Ocean

Map Key
____ state boundary
---- national boundary

1. Put an **X** on a label, a title, and an inset map.   Answers will vary.

2. Name the states shown in the inset maps.

   _____Alaska_____   _____Hawaii_____

3. Circle the places below that are labeled on the map.

   (oceans)   mountains   continents

   river   hills   lake

   plains   (states)   (national capital)

Geography Themes Up Close

Regions share something that makes them different from other places. A region can have the same kinds of plants. Regions can be big or small.

This is a **chart**. It shows facts in a way that is easy to read. This chart shows the kinds of plants and animals in three regions.

Regions	Plants	Animals
	trees, bushes, moss	goats, sheep, bears
	trees, grasses	deer, rabbits, squirrels, birds
	seaweeds	fish, shellfish, whales, dolphins

1. In which region does moss grow?

   _____mountain region_____

2. What animals live in plains regions?

   _____deer, rabbits, squirrels, birds_____

3. What plants grow in ocean regions?

   _____seaweeds_____

A neighborhood can be a region. A neighborhood has places for people to live, work, and play.

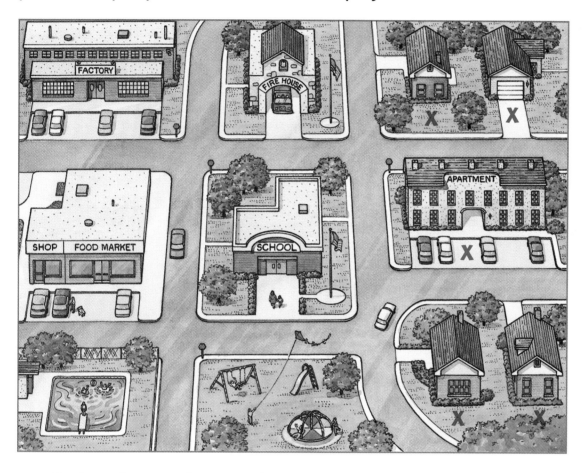

4. Find a place to live on the map. Mark an **X** below it.

5. Name a place in the neighborhood where people work.

   shop, food market, factory, school, apartments, park, pool
   _____

6. Find places to play. Which of these places do you have in your neighborhood?

   Answers will vary, but will probably include pool, park, playground, yards.

   _____

The United States

Map Key

| national capital | ⊛ | national capital |
| state capital | ★ | state capital |

national boundary — ·— ·—

state boundary ——

Russia

Canada

Alaska

Canada

Juneau ★

Arctic Ocean

Pacific Ocean

Washington
★ Olympia
Salem ★

Oregon

Idaho
★ Boise

Nevada
Carson City ★

California

Sacramento ★

Montana
Helena ★

Wyoming
Cheyenne ★

Utah
Salt Lake City ★

Arizona
★ Phoenix

Colorado
Denver ★

New Mexico
★ Santa Fe

North Dakota
★ Bismarck

South Dakota
★ Pierre

Nebraska
Lincoln ★

Kansas
Topeka ★

Oklahoma
Oklahoma City ★

Texas
Austin ★

Mexico

Minnesota
St. Paul ★

Iowa
Des Moines ★

Missouri
Jefferson City ★

Arkansas
Little Rock ★

Louisiana
Baton Rouge ★

Wisconsin
Madison ★

Lake Superior

Lake Michigan

Michigan
Lansing ★

Illinois
Springfield ★

Indiana
Indianapolis ★

Kentucky
Frankfort ★

Tennessee
Nashville ★

Mississippi
Jackson ★

Alabama
Montgomery ★

Lake Huron

Lake Erie

Ohio
Columbus ★

West Virginia
Charleston ★

Lake Ontario

Pennsylvania
Harrisburg ★

Virginia
Richmond ★

North Carolina
Raleigh ★

South Carolina
Columbia ★

Georgia
Atlanta ★

Florida
Tallahassee ★

Maine
Augusta ★

Vermont
Montpelier ★

New Hampshire
Concord ★

Massachusetts
Boston ★

Rhode Island
Providence ★

Connecticut
Hartford ★

New York
Albany ★

New Jersey
Trenton ★

Delaware
Dover ★

Washington, D.C.

Maryland
Annapolis ★ ⊛

Atlantic Ocean

Gulf of Mexico

Hawaii
Honolulu ★

Pacific Ocean

Pacific Ocean

Arctic Ocean

Greenland

(U.S.)

Canada

Hudson
Bay

Pacific Ocean

Ottawa ✪

Great
Lakes

United States

Washington, D.C. ✪

Atlantic Ocean

Gulf of Mexico

Bahamas

U.S.
Virgin
Islands

Mexico

Cuba

Haiti

Puerto
Rico

Jamaica

Dominican
Republic

Mexico City ✪

Caribbean Sea

Belize

Guatemala

Honduras

El Salvador

Nicaragua

Costa Rica

Panama

N
W E
S

North America

Atlas **61**

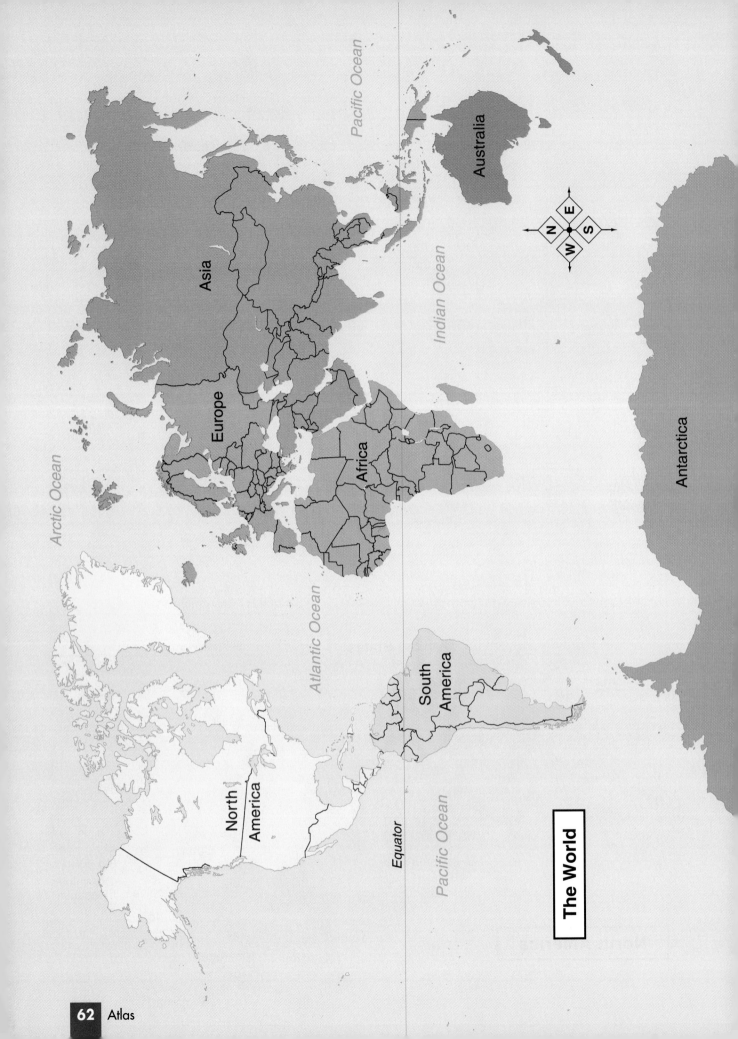

Pacific Ocean

Australia

Asia

N E
W S

Europe

Indian Ocean

Africa

Arctic Ocean

Antarctica

Atlantic Ocean

South
America

North
America

Pacific Ocean

Equator

The World

Glossary

boundary (p. 44) the dividing line on a map where one place begins and another place ends

capital city (p. 45) a place where laws are made for a state or country

chart (p. 58) facts shown in a way that is easy to read

compass rose (p. 23) a symbol that shows the directions: north, south, east, and west

continent (p. 30) the largest landforms. There are seven continents on Earth.

directions (p. 22) the four directions are north, south, east, and west

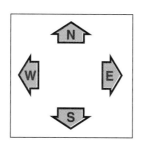

Equator (p. 31) the imaginary line around the middle of Earth

globe (p. 30) a model of Earth

grid (p. 43) lines that cross each other to make squares

hill (p. 9) land that rises above the land around it

human/environment interaction (pp. 5, 14) tells how people live, work, and play on Earth. It tells how people use the land.

inset map (p. 53) a special box on a main map with a smaller map inside

island (p. 8) land with water all around it

label (p. 52) a word that names a place on a map or a globe

lake (p. 8) a body of water with land all around it

location (p. 4, 42) tells where something is found on Earth

map (p. 17) a drawing of a real place. A map shows the place from above.

map key (p. 17) the guide that tells what the symbols on a map stand for

mountain (p. 9) land that rises higher than a hill

movement (p. 6, 28) how people, goods, and ideas get from one place to another

national boundary (p. 45) the dividing line on a map between nations or countries

national capital (p. 45) a place where laws are made for a nation or country

ocean (p. 9) the largest body of water on Earth

photo (p. 16) a picture made by a camera

place (p. 5, 50) tells what a location is like

plain (p. 9) flat land that is good for farming

regions (p. 7, 58) parts of Earth that are alike

river (p. 8) a large stream of water that flows into a larger body of water

state boundary (p. 45) the dividing line on a map between states

symbol (p. 17) a picture on a map. It stands for something real.

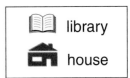

title (p. 53) the name of a map

valley (p. 8) a low place between higher land